HILDEGARD
of Bingen

a spiritual reader

HILDEGARD
of Bingen

CARMEN ACEVEDO BUTCHER

PARACLETE PRESS
Brewster, Massachusetts

Hildegard of Bingen: A Spiritual Reader

2007 First Printing

ISBN 13: 978-155725-490-0

Library of Congress Cataloging-in-Publication Data
Butcher, Carmen Acevedo.
    Hildegard of Bingen: a spiritual reader / Carmen Acevedo Butcher.
        p. cm.
    Includes bibliographical references.
    ISBN 978-1-55725-490-0
    1. Hildegard, Saint, 1098-1179. 2. Mysticism—Germany—History—
Middle Ages, 600-1500—Sources. 3. Mysticism—Early works to 1800.
4. Christian women saints—Religious life. I. Hildegard, Saint, 1098-
1179. II. Title.
    BX4700.H5B88 2007
    282.092—dc22   2006033729

10 9 8 7 6 5 4 3 2 1

Published by Paraclete Press
Brewster, Massachusetts
www.paracletepress.com

Printed in the United States of America

This book is dedicated to the late
Frau Sophie Buschbeck, née Schott

Mother Buschbeck was born in Geischen, Silesia, in 1905, and left earth eighty-seven years later, *"aus einem reich erfüllten Leben in die Ewigkeit abgerufen"* ("called from a rich, full life into eternity"). Her spirit was cut from the same cloth as Hildegard's. One strangely cold November, she made me apple-scrap tea and gave me a relative's thick wool turtleneck to replace my acrylic one. I was the homesick twenty-two-year-old student for whom she cooked a hot American-style lunch every Friday. She continued showing me *si vere Deum quaerit* ("sincerity in seeking God") when she answered every question sent from Georgia in cramped black ink on the thinnest paper in a decade-high stack of blue airmail envelopes. For each of these gifts, *Mutti, danke schön.*

Let your eye live and grow in God,
and your soul will never shrivel.
You can count on it to keep you alive . . . awake . . . tender.
—Hildegard, *Letter to Archbishop Arnold of Mainz*

Humanity, take a good look at yourself.
Inside, you've got heaven and earth, and all of creation.
You're a world—everything is hidden in you.
—Hildegard, *Causes and Cures*

When a person does something wrong and the soul realizes this, the
deed is like poison in the soul. Conversely, a good deed is as sweet
to the soul as delicious food is to the body. The soul circulates
through the body like sap through a tree, maturing a person the
way sap helps a tree turn green and grow flowers and fruit.
—Hildegard, *Scivias*

Don't let yourself forget that God's grace rewards not only those
who never slip, but also those who bend and fall. So sing! The song
of rejoicing softens hard hearts. It makes tears of godly sorrow flow
from them. Singing summons the Holy Spirit. Happy praises
offered in simplicity and love lead the faithful to complete harmony,
without discord. Don't stop singing.
—Hildegard, *Scivias*

CONTENTS

MAP OF HILDEGARD'S GERMANY   x

PREFACE   xi

THE LIFE OF HILDEGARD   1

1: Songs   23

2: *Scivias* (*Know the Ways of the Lord*)   49

3: *The Play of the Virtues*   69

4: Selections from Her Letters   95

5: *Physica* and *Causes and Cures*   127

6: *The Book of Life's Merits*   135

7: *The Book of Divine Works*   149

CONCLUSION   159

ACKNOWLEDGMENTS   161

APPENDIX A: Chronology of Hildegard's Life   163

APPENDIX B: Further Reading Material and Recordings of Hildegard's Music   171

NOTES   179

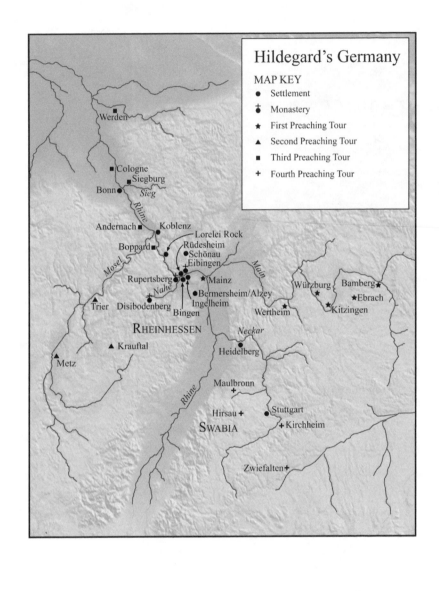

Hildegard's Germany

MAP KEY

● Settlement
☥ Monastery
★ First Preaching Tour
▲ Second Preaching Tour
■ Third Preaching Tour
+ Fourth Preaching Tour

Werden

Cologne
Siegburg
Bonn
Sieg
Rhine

Andernach   Koblenz
                        Lorelei Rock
Boppard   Rüdesheim
                  Schönau
                  Eibingen
Rupertsberg   Mainz
Mosel   Nahe   Bermersheim/Alzey   Würzburg   Bamberg
Trier Disibodenberg   Ingelheim   Ebrach
                  Bingen   Wertheim   Kitzingen
RHEINHESSEN   Main

                  Neckar
Krauftal
Metz   Heidelberg

Rhine   Maulbronn
                        +
            Hirsau +   Stuttgart
            SWABIA   + Kirchheim

                  Zwiefalten +

PREFACE

She is a remarkable woman in an age of remarkable men.
—Christopher Page, in an interview[1]

*W*HY PAUL MCCARTNEY AND STEVIE WONDER, John Mellencamp, the Steve Miller Band, and Chicago didn't drown it out is anybody's guess. What could possibly be heard over "Ebony and Ivory," "Jack and Diane," "Abracadabra," and "Hard for Me to Say I'm Sorry"? And who could have known that an unlooked-for debut recording of unknown pre-classical music by an obscure medieval nun would conquer the *Billboard* classical charts and start a Hildegard revolution?

But that's just what happened twenty-five years ago when Christopher Page and his Gothic Voices group recorded *A Feather on the Breath of God*, winning a Gramophone award and selling a quarter of a million copies. More people than ever before began to find their way to Hildegard. Today, her music and her books have an international audience, hundreds of websites are devoted to her, videos have been made about her, a publishing company is named after her, and people gather all over the world to discuss her work. The only downside to Hildegard's modern celebrity is that her original-yet-orthodox self has been appropriated by many camps. New Age reformers invoke her name over crystals, and feminists see her as their Mother. What is it about Hildegard's work that invites us all in? And who is she really?

This book tries to answer those questions, or at least to suggest that Hildegard is a complex woman with a unique voice, and also very much a product of her time. The words that fill these pages are not literal translations that skewer art with their precise woodenness. Instead, I tried to let Hildegard's poems sing with double and triple meanings as they do in the Latin, and to let her sometimes strange prose hint at otherworldly messages so weighty that they crush mere words and make them buckle as you read them. Writing this book has been a year-long *lectio divina* for me, nourishing and challenging my soul, and I hope the result will guide you to the essential in her—something like a "Hildegard 101," because, if my own reaction is anything to go by, the world is ripe for an authentic word from this tenacious Benedictine nun.

In this endeavor, I have read and worked with the vast scholarly literature available on Hildegard, and my debt to those who have gone before me is both immense and inspiring. Unless otherwise noted, the translations are my own, and they show that Hildegard is indeed the best example of the so-called "Renaissance of the twelfth century." As such, she deserves the gritty, vibrant, and sinewy contemporary voice you will find in these pages. Her most representative, most stunning ideas are offered here in a language that we can all understand. Whoever you are, first-time Hildegard reader or long-time Hildegard friend—I hope that discovering her works distilled in this book will stir and awaken your soul, as it did mine, in profoundly gentle ways.

I started this reader, asking: *How can I get a handle on Hildegard?* Trying to answer that question proved as challenging as trying to move thirteen large-to-bursting suitcases through a packed airport en route to a foreign land, with two small children in tow—an experience my husband, Sean, and I chose when we wanted to get better acquainted with our Korean son's birth country. Likewise, as I grappled with Hildegard's profound writings on a journey into the mystery of God, they revealed their resistance to easy organization and facile lifting. Her descriptions of and engagement with the "divine living Light" required idea-bursting, ever-shifting paradoxes and an awareness that embracing life's heft (whether spiritual or Samsonite) is possible only in community.

My family's long trip into the otherness of Korea began one hot, sticky summer afternoon when my parents gave us and our children hugs to last a year and left us at the Atlanta airport, where Sean and I stood rooted to the spot, staring at those bags. *They'd grown since we'd left home, hadn't they?* But my husband found a cart, and on it we stacked, restacked, and stacked again bags that slipped, slid, and generally collided. Finally a porter helped us. With two hands, she heaved each suitcase up on the outsized four-wheel trolley, shoving them one by one into a tilting pile more fluid than I expected heavy-duty-polyester-fabric-with-push-button-locking-handles-and-inline-skate-wheels could be. One of us was forever massaging this mound back into place as she rolled us through the crowded airport and directly to the right check-in counter.

Hildegard's Mt.-Everest-sized lifework also expands under close examination. Take one pebble of an example—the Latin in her ground-breaking allegorical musical, *Ordo virtutum* (*The Play of the Virtues*). This work uses words chosen skillfully for their many different levels of meaning, words that sink into the heart and then grow, like good poetry, or, to continue with a Hildegardian garden metaphor, like fertile seeds. This pioneering musical opens with a chorus of Old Testament Patriarchs and Prophets singing to the personified New Testament virtues (such as Humility and Charity): "We're the roots, and . . . you're the apple of the living eye."

This line is richer when we know why Hildegard picked the Latin *oculus* for "eye" in "the living eye" above. In addition to its anatomical meaning, *oculus* has the botanical definition of a leaf, shoot, or flower bud. With one carefully selected word, Hildegard has set up a complex image: The patriarchs and prophets who prefigured and predicted Christ were the "roots" of God's divine tree, on which sprouted the most delicate "bud," who is God's Son, and from Him grew the "fruit" of the virtues: Humility, Charity, Divine Love, Patience, and their sisters. This is a favorite metaphor for Hildegard, and in her songs she praises the Virgin Mary as the "twig" or "branch" on which the "bud," baby Jesus, flowered. By her intelligent selection of this one word, *oculus*, Hildegard has shown the center of her work—that to see God is to grow.

This example also suggests the complexity of Hildegard's work. Would you expect anything less from an abbess/artist/cosmologist/composer/counselor/dietitian/dramatist/epistoler/healer/linguist /mystic/naturalist/philosopher/poet/political consultant/preacher/prophet/visionary who wrote theological, naturalistic, botanical, medicinal, and dietary texts, as well as letters, liturgical songs, poems, and the play, while supervising brilliant miniature illuminations? My pilgrimage through Hildegard's works quickly convinced me that "getting a handle" on her is not the objective. Luggage is one thing, but who can lift a mountain?

Instead, I followed a gentle path up through her art, deciding on a fairly chronological route, fully aware that what I was doing was somewhat artificial, because Hildegard's creativity never marched down an a-b-c-d, 1-2-3 path. She was always engaged on more than one front and in more than one genre, and she also loved to mix genres, writing music and poems contemporaneously with letters, books, and a play, while supervising wonderful manuscript illuminations; and she includes songs and sermons in her letters, while her visionary works are filled, not just with visions, but also with parables. I have tried to give these many works a memorable symmetry by consciously imposing on them a hopefully useful "start"-to-"finish." For light along the path, I recommend keeping a copy of Hildegard's vibrant, brilliant illuminations on the bedside table, such as the readily available *Illuminations of Hildegard of Bingen* by Matthew Fox.[2]

We start with the lyrics of her songs, which are some of the best, even the most "modern" poems of the twelfth century. Like many students of Hildegard, I knew her music before I knew her prose or her illuminations. This is apt, because harmony seems to be Hildegard's own starting point. Her earliest spiritual experiences were spent chanting the Benedictine *Opus Dei*, which puts plainsong at the center of her spiritual walk. Singing was her way to God.

Her music is also a splendid introduction to the themes resonating in her rich and varied corpus. We may not be able to give her musical compositions precise dates, but we do know that she was writing music in the 1140s and that a copy of her seventy-plus liturgical songs, the *Symphonia*, existed and was being sung in 1155 in the monastic churches at Rupertsberg, at Disibod, at Trier, and perhaps at another church or two outside Germany. Since her songs represent some of her earliest, most memorable, and most engaging creations, they open this book, with recommended recordings given in the second appendix.

Next, we stop to explore *Scivias*, Hildegard's first major theological text and the most cogent expression of her basic beliefs. She completed this prose work in 1151, after ten years of dogged writing. *Scivias* concludes with an early version of Hildegard's musical, *The Play of the Virtues*, which is the third stop on our journey. My students love this frequently overlooked but increasingly performed work, perhaps because it presents Hildegard's *leitmotif* in a straightforward, exciting manner (and also because we act it out in class). This theme is that God the Father loves us, every soul is given free will, the resurrected Christ is our redeemer, and the Holy Spirit renews us and all creation, so we can love each other.

Then we wind through Hildegard's expressive letters to powerful kings and humble monks before reaching her medical and natural history works. While her letters are mostly straightforward, her "scientific" and "medical" writings may sometimes seem peculiar to the modern mind, although their notions were easily accepted by and totally familiar to a medieval audience. In them, she even discusses human sexuality in a way that suggests she must have counseled many lay women and also meditated on this subject at length.

At this point in our adventure through the writings of this Benedictine nun, we encounter her dazzling, sometimes puzzling, but always fascinating final major theological books, *The Book of Life's Merits* and *The Book of Divine Works*. When we finish exploring these, we have (to my mind) reached the summit. Our trek is complete.

But "the end is where we start from," as T. S. Eliot observes in "Little Gidding," and I hope that the chronology of Hildegard's life in the first appendix, plus the other resources and recordings listed at the back, will guide the curious reader further down the path, just as the Hartsfield-Jackson porter helped us en route to our foreign destination. Hildegard and every seeker-of-God know from experience that the very nature of the soul is a forever-beginning. Her mentor St. Benedict admits this when he ends his profoundly wise *Rule* by saying that it was written for "beginners." Or, as Mother Buschbeck used to tell me in Heidelberg, and I remember to this day: *"Es gibt kein Ende der geistlichen Reise; man kann immer weiter gehen."* ("There's no end to the spiritual journey. We can always go further.")

THE LIFE of HILDEGARD

I am more convinced than ever that [Hildegard]
still remains to be appreciated, not only as an inspiration
for the present age but also as one of the most complex,
significant, and fascinating creators and transmitters
of her own twelfth-century culture.
—Barbara Newman, *Sister of Wisdom:*
St. Hildegard's Theology of the Feminine[3]

ETWEEN THE SUMMER OF 1098 AND THE AUTUMN OF 1179, a remarkable German woman lived eighty-one years at a time when half that long was considered a full life. The Über-multitasking *Frau*, this Benedictine nun founded two convents; organized the first-ever public preaching tours conducted by a woman; authored nearly four hundred bold letters to popes, emperors, abbesses, abbots, monks, nuns, and laypeople; worked as healer, naturalist, botanist, dietary specialist, and exorcist; composed daring music; crafted poetry with staying power; wrote the first surviving sung morality play; and spent decades writing three compelling theological works. Meet the incomparable Hildegard of Bingen. Her long resume is impressive in any age, but it pales when compared with her life, which she considered her best divine offering.

A thorough knowledge of the way Hildegard lived is essential to understanding her other creations.

The woman long famous now as the "Sibyl of the Rhine" was born the youngest child of ten in a noble family in the then-anonymous village of Bermersheim, twelve miles southwest of Mainz. From the start, her destiny was inextricably linked with this beautiful middle Rhine River valley, the area of western Germany known as the *Rheinhessen*. Tourists visit each year to enjoy its gentle emerald hills, terraced vineyards, and medieval castles.

I was once one of these visitors. In the early 1980s, I left Heidelberg on the first morning train heading north to Bonn, following the Rhine River up. I was twenty-three and abroad for the first time as a Rotary Club International scholar. A professor at my undergraduate college had introduced me to Hildegard two years earlier, and it thrilled me to realize that Hildegard would have passed through this same gorgeous countryside more than eight centuries earlier. I was gawking out the window when my traveling companion poked me, promising, *"Später erzähle ich Dir die Sage von der Lorelei."* This was Frau Sophie Buschbeck, my seventy-nine-year-old friend. Her explosive German syllables let me know that later, when we came on the right spot, she wanted to tell me the legend of the Lorelei, a sheer rock cliff famous for the hypnotic singing of its beautiful maiden.

En route, Mother Buschbeck explained that the Lorelei had long marked the narrowest bend in the Rhine River between the North Sea and Switzerland. This narrowness, plus a dangerously strong current and plenty of underwater rocks, once triggered many boat accidents. When we finally clickety-clacked past that gray-green rock rising 400 feet straight up out of the shimmering river into the azure sky, Mother Buschbeck began reciting the spine-tingling legend as penned by the nineteenth-century poet Heinrich Heine:

The most beautiful woman is sitting on the Lorelei rock. She's amazing—look at her! Her golden jewelry sparkling as she combs her golden hair, she combs it with a golden comb, and—as she combs—she sings a unique melody that's simply overpowering!

I thought then and still think now how fitting it is that Hildegard's magnificent life and harmonious writings and compositions are connected with an area renowned for its stunning beauty and for the irresistible power of singing.

A Toddler's Visions, and a Human Tithe

Hildegard's spiritual journey began early, with her first vision at three. Two years later, she looked at a pregnant cow and predicted the color markings of its future calf, scaring her nurse. Too young to understand these revelations, and most likely scared herself, Hildegard hid this gift for years. Her parents, however, noticed her spiritual strengths and supported her life's mission by giving their tenth child to the church as a tithe. They may have also decided to do this because of Hildegard's susceptibility to illness. They probably believed the monastic life would protect and strengthen their daughter's never-quite-robust health. At eight, then, Hildegard began her spiritual quest in earnest when she was willingly committed to the religious life by her devout parents.

Two of Hildegard's brothers and one of her sisters also dedicated themselves to the Church: Hugh became choirmaster of Mainz cathedral; Roric, a canon in Tholey; and Clementia, a nun at Hildegard's Rupertsberg. Drutwin was the oldest brother and first heir, and there were three other sisters, Odilia, Irmengard, and Jutta. That leaves two siblings unaccounted for. Perhaps they died in childhood.

Compared with the names given to her known brothers and sisters, Hildegard's own moniker seems most prophetic. When her parents

Hildebert and Mechthilde chose *Hildegard*, they were obviously giving their daughter a piece of their own names. All contain the Old Germanic word *hild*, for "battle" or "fight." Hildegard's father's name means "battle *fortress* (*bert*)," while her mother's translates "*powerful or strong* (*mecht*) in battle." *Hildegard* literally signifies "a *place* (*gard*) of battle," implying strength in fighting. In other words, *Hildegard* is just the name you would want to give your daughter if you wanted her to be a spiritual warrior. Hildegard's younger friend, the mystic Elisabeth of Schönau (1129–65), recognized this eponymic significance and wrote her about it in a letter: "My lady Hildegard, how fitting it is that you are named *Hildegard*, because through you God *protects* his church in spiritual *conflicts*."[4]

But very earthly "holy wars" plagued her day, just as they do our own. Hildegard was a baby when the first, "triumphant" crusade took place. Pope Urban II's crusaders besieged Jerusalem for five bloody weeks before taking it in the summer of 1099, massacring its every citizen. Later, Bernard of Clairvaux (1090–1153) traveled through northern France, Flanders, and the Rhine area, speaking to enthusiastic crowds and drumming up support for a second crusade. Hildegard's life and his crossed paths more than once as she sought papal approval for her preaching. The German Emperor Frederick Barbarossa, whom Hildegard wrote when she felt he needed correction, distinguished himself in this second "doomed" crusade, but ten years after Hildegard's death, Barbarossa joined the third crusade and drowned on June 10, 1190, as he attempted to cross the Saleph River in the Roman province of Cilicia, never making it to the Holy Land.

While the crusaders sought to conquer by the sword, Hildegard focused instead on God's love. Her work shows how each of us can spiritually engage the battle within the soul, by finding the Benedictine balance of prayer and work, by recognizing God's creativity in the physical and spiritual mysteries of each human, by accepting Christ's never-ending mercy, and by rejecting corruption within the Church and in secular politics.

When Hildegard was fourteen, she moved from her childhood home in Bermersheim, traveling some fourteen miles due west to the St. Disibod Abbey at Disibodenberg. On All Saints' Day, November 1, 1112, she was given over as an oblate into the care of Jutta of Spanheim, the daughter of Count Stephen of Spanheim, an aristocratic anchoress only six years Hildegard's elder. Jutta was also related to Marchioness Richardis of Stade, the mother of the Archbishop Hartwig of Bremen and of the Richardis who was intimate friends with Hildegard.

These upper-class connections remind us that Hildegard was no waif left on the convent stoop. Hildegard's aristocratic background prepared her to act boldly on the world stage. This future boldness was grounded, however, in the listening quiet of Hildegard's earliest Benedictine years.

Jutta and young Hildegard lived together in a cell attached to the monastery of St. Disibod. Jutta taught Hildegard to write; to read the collection of psalms used in the liturgy; and to chant the *Opus Dei* ("work of God"), the weekly sequential recitation of the Latin Psalter. She probably also taught Hildegard to play the zitherlike stringed instrument called the psaltery.

The vibrant Hildegard may have sewed or embroidered her way through these teenage years, devoting herself to the traditional "weaving" activities approved-by-males for female monastics. During this time of relative isolation, Hildegard ate a simple but nourishing diet of eggs, soup, cheese, bread, beans, and fruit. These were passed to the hermits through a window specifically designed for that purpose, and their wastes were passed out the same window. Jutta and

Hildegard were not allowed to come and go at leisure, and this confinement must have been difficult at times for this visionary young woman.

Hildegard's dedication to the Church was viewed as the most serious commitment. Part of the dedication ceremony included the last rites (today called the Sacrament of the Anointing of the Sick and the Viaticum). The anchoress-to-be lay on a bier to receive extreme unction in case she became mortally ill in the future. Early in her life, then, Hildegard was seen as dying to this world with its mundane earthly concerns and living only for God.

Jutta's Bruising Asceticism

Jutta herself may have added challenges to these early monastic years. She was a severe practitioner of asceticism, including penitential self-flagellation. She wore a chain under her clothes, prayed barefoot in the extreme cold of a German winter, and refused the allowed (and even encouraged) modifications to the Benedictine diet for those who were sick. As an adult, Hildegard would teach moderation. Perhaps her experiences as a wide-eyed youth watching her earliest companion and teacher suffer extreme penance made Hildegard embrace balance in this practice. When Jutta died in 1136 at forty-four, Hildegard did not react with passion to this loss, and we can wonder how close they really were, despite their intimate proximity over three decades.

But Hildegard clearly loved her other primary teacher, the St. Disibod monk Volmar. He acted as prior and father confessor for the nuns at Disibodenberg. As a teenager, Hildegard began to realize her visions were unique experiences, and she broke her painful silence by discussing them with Jutta, who told Volmar. Volmar, in turn, became the first person to validate Hildegard's visions. He also mentored her for a time. Volmar recognized Hildegard's rare spiritual talents and later became her secretary and good friend. Although both Jutta and Volmar were Hildegard's first confidants, Hildegard became especially close to this monk.

She needed mentors, for Hildegard was a great self-doubter. Her two biggest insecurities and concomitant strengths stem from the informal schooling of her childhood and from the way she kept her visions bottled up in herself. She constantly lamented her lack of formal education and spent years seeking confirmation from the Church for her divine visions. She also consciously referred to herself in her work as "*ego paupercula feminea forma*," meaning "I, in the inferior form of a woman." Even after allowing for the classic rhetoric of such "I-am-unworthy" pleas, and taking into consideration Hildegard's genuine need to gain papal approval for the ongoing success of her ministry in a male-dominated culture that regarded woman as a lower species, the twenty-first-century reader senses in this powerful German prophet a fascinating, deeply insecure awareness of self.

Hildegard's profound self-doubting was, however, the very root of her vibrancy, because it was matched with an equally acute certainty in God the merciful and the mysterious. The English Romantic poet John Keats called this tendency "Negative Capability," when a person "is capable of being in uncertainties, mysteries, doubts, without any irritable reaching after fact and reason."[5] In other words, Hildegard had the soul of a poet in everything she did.

These unique frailties informed her greatest strengths, and Hildegard also used them rhetorically to great advantage. Although she was obviously well-read in the liturgy (and through it, the Scriptures), the *Benedictine Rule*, the writings of the early Church Fathers, and perhaps even some Classical texts, Hildegard always claimed to have been taught by an "*indocte mulier*" ("unlearned woman"). She had not been through the formal, males-only training of the *artes liberales*. The core curriculum for the ancient liberal arts program included the medieval *trivium* of grammar, rhetoric, and dialectic, a course of study very similar to majoring in classical literature at a university today, and then the *quadrivium* of music, arithmetic, geometry, and astronomy. But, all of this excluded the female student.

Hildegard accepted her pedagogical deficiency with the wisdom of Paul's second letter to the Corinthians: "He [Jesus] said to me, 'My grace is sufficient for you, for power is made perfect in weakness.' So, I will boast all the more gladly of my weaknesses, so that the power of Christ may dwell in me."[6] With this paradoxical truth in mind, Hildegard reminded her audience repeatedly that her visions and her counsel had obviously originated in divine inspiration, precisely because she had no formal training in such. Who could argue with that logic? She added that God had chosen her, a woman and the weakest, to speak because the times were so "sissy" (literally "woman-ish")! Hildegard was suggesting that men had made such a mess of things that God had to call a "weak woman" in to save the day. That reasoning is how Hildegard turned what she and others of her day perceived as an educational and gender-specific weakness into a huge spiritual asset.

Most important, this Benedictine nun's forever-shifting analysis of herself was the "crack" that allowed in a solid, confident sense of God's mystery. Her need drank God in. The result was Hildegard's dynamic, creative mind and her powerfully visionary soul. These energize her writings and her every artistic and practical accomplishment.

The same logic applies to Hildegard's untrained, unpolished Latin. She made a masculine Church speak her own tongue. She turned it (sometimes accidentally) into exactly what her original visions required—a unique language. Her style is as unsystematic and as organic as her theology. Hildegard liked piling clause on clause, and her grammar can be less-than-exact; but even her most inelegant sentences have a rough beauty that communicates the power of her other-worldly revelations and their multiple meanings. Both messy and fecund—the way of every creative process, whether a volcanic eruption or a baby's birth—Hildegard's Latin style creates memorable challenges for the English translator. Her plays on words give her writings another layer of meaning resisting translation.

But why did Hildegard choose to write in Latin? Why not German? A century earlier, across the water in Anglo-Saxon England, the Benedictine monk Ælfric (c. 955–c. 1010) decided to write most of his sermons in his native Old English. He even translated much of the Bible into this vernacular language. Hildegard's writings would have been quite different, and possibly even more exciting, had she written them in the German of her day, with its rich capacity for passionate and philosophical expression. She chose Latin for entirely practical reasons. First, it gave her writings, and especially their *female* author, the Church authority they required; second, as the transmitted language of the time, Latin ensured that her works would be passed on to future generations; and finally, Hildegard's target audience was the upper class, who read Latin.

Hildegard's Coming of Age

During Jutta and Hildegard's days together, they attracted others who wanted to follow God. By the time Jutta died when Hildegard was in her late thirties, their anchoresses' cell had morphed into a small Benedictine monastery. Jutta's death opened the way for the nuns to elect Hildegard as her successor, and only five years after Jutta's death, Hildegard received the prophetic call to write down her visions for the world to read. We can speculate much about the effect that the death of Hildegard's earliest spiritual mentor had on her. It may have been the most crucial point in her life, because it seems to have allowed Hildegard's soul to stand up straight. If Hildegard's silence on this relationship with her first teacher is any indication, Jutta's strong influence was not always salutary, and if Jutta had lived on and on, we can wonder if her pupil would have been able to break out into her own psychic space as vigorously as she did.

Hildegard tells us that when she was aged forty-two God commanded her to write down and publish what she had seen and heard in her soul. That was in 1141. The book would much later become her first visionary work, *Scivias*. But Hildegard did not begin immediately. She hesitated, doubting her ability to serve as God's prophet. Medieval society judged women unworthy to write. Writing was manly. When Hildegard became sick from her self-doubt, she analyzed her illness as a sign that her disobedience had upset God, so she turned to her teacher and friend Volmar and told him everything. He encouraged her to obey the vision's bright commandment, "Write." Finally she began a ten-year writing effort that would bring her much contemporary recognition.

Today the divine authority of Hildegard's voice is universally recognized, but near the middle of the twelfth century, she had still not received the coveted papal seal of approval. In 1147, Hildegard wrote Bernard of Clairvaux in an attempt to get the Church to validate her visions. She describes herself to him in the usual manner as "worthless, and even more than worthless with the name of woman" but adds that—despite her weaknesses, sicknesses, fears, and uncertainties— she is certain her visions are good and divine.

Meanwhile, Volmar was campaigning on her behalf. He told Abbot Kuno of St. Disibod about his student's visions, the abbot told the archbishop of Mainz, and the archbishop mentioned Hildegard to Pope Eugenius III, who was at the 1147-48 synod in nearby Trier. A disciple of Bernard of Clairvaux, the pope sent representatives to St. Disibod to visit Hildegard. They came back with a copy of the unfinished *Scivias* manuscript, and the Pope himself read from this document to the synod's clergymen and dignitaries, who applauded.

Letters suggest that Pope Eugenius may have read from the first two stunning visions of *Scivias*'s second book. The text he read so impressed the assembly (among whom was Bernard of Clairvaux) that the Pope wrote to Hildegard, commanding her to keep on writing. Papal approval jump-started Hildegard's career as a public intellectual and spiritual leader. Without it, she would probably have been censured eventually by some churchman for transgressing the prohibitions against public female expression, as written down in the fourteenth chapter of the New Testament epistle 1 Corinthians.[7] Even with the approval of His Holiness, it still took Hildegard ten more years to finish *Scivias*.

While she was working on the *Scivias* manuscript, Hildegard founded her first abbey. The Disibodenberg monks vehemently opposed this new foundation. They would lose much both spiritually and financially when Hildegard took her community and left. Even some of Hildegard's own nuns balked at abandoning Disibod for what they knew to be a desolate location and significant hardship.

But Hildegard was unstoppable when she felt her mandate was from God, and in 1150, with the support of the elder Richardis of Stade (who had contacted Archbishop Heinrich I of Mainz), Hildegard took some twenty nuns and went nineteen miles northeast to Rupertsberg ("Mt. Rupert"), overlooking Bingen at the juncture of the Rhine River and the River Nahe. She was determined to build a new community on the ruins there of a Carolingian monastery—her *Vita* explains that she was told to do so in a vision. It took Hildegard many more years of wrangling with Abbot Kuno and the

Disibodenberg monks before she successfully disentangled the finances of her new convent from those of St. Disibod. Her eventual success was linked to the fact that Hildegard was well-connected.

One year after relocating her community to Rupertsberg, and only a few years after the important 1147-48 synod, Hildegard finished dictating *Scivias* to Volmar, the prior of her new Rupertsberg community, and to the nun Richardis of Stade, her other close friend, whom she called her "daughter." During this time, Hildegard was also supervising the construction of buildings for her new monastery. We can picture her walking through the noisy construction site that was Rupertsberg and perhaps contemplating a title for her first major visionary work.

The twenty-six intense visions that became Hildegard's *Scivias* are illuminated by thirty-five equally bold miniatures. Hildegard knew the art of illumination and probably supervised the design and creation of these in her own scriptorium at the new abbey of Rupertsberg. The illuminated paintings are done in a fresh, naïf style, not unlike Hildegard's own peculiar, intense, and grammatically loose Latin. What the miniatures lack in formal polish is more than compensated by their bold colors and designs.

The Daring Musician

A multi-faceted artist, Hildegard was not only an author and a talented visual designer, but a musician of note. Her allegiance to God through her music is one of the strongest refrains in her life. She believed music was necessary for salvation, because it was the best representation of the state of humanity before the Fall. If a person wanted to know what it felt like to be alive before the Fall, Hildegard believed holy music could take you there, as she writes in her famous letter to the Prelates of Mainz:

Music stirs our hearts and engages our souls in ways we can't describe. When this happens, we are taken beyond our earthly banishment back to the divine melody Adam knew when he sang with the angels, when he was whole in God, before his exile. In fact, before Adam refused God's fragrant flower of obedience, his voice was the best on earth, because he was made by God's green thumb, who is the Holy Spirit. And if Adam had never lost the harmony God first gave him, the mortal fragilities that we all possess today could never have survived hearing the booming resonance of that original voice.

By the late 1140s, when Hildegard was well into the writing of *Scivias*, she was already known for her original liturgical music celebrating God the Father, His Son, the Holy Spirit, Mary and her Son, the Church, heavenly music, and the saints, but this twelfth-century polymath never restricted herself to involvement in just one activity. Musician, abbess, writer—she also worked as a political consultant. She was the kind of woman who could be invited to the German Emperor's palace at Ingelheim, and would go and make a lasting good impression. This meeting took place soon after Frederick Barbarossa was crowned Emperor in 1155. While there, Hildegard must have been asked to prophesy for the Emperor, because he later wrote her about this meeting:

> We write to notify you, holy lady, that your predictions came true, exactly as you said they would when we invited you to our court at Ingelheim. With all our might, we will work to honor our kingdom. Dear lady, we ask that you continue to pray for us, and the sisters, too, that we will know God's grace.

Not long after their encounter, Emperor Barbarossa granted Hildegard's Rupertsberg convent an edict of imperial protection in perpetuity. From then on, whenever the Emperor ordered attacks on certain monasteries supporting the Roman pope, Hildegard's convent was always spared. This special protection did not, however, stop Abbess Hildegard from writing Frederick harsh letters of rebuke when he appointed anti-popes (including, on one occasion, calling him "a totally insane man"). Her first allegiance was always to her heavenly Emperor.

The Busy Sixty-Something Nun

Throughout her life, Hildegard continued to find new artistic and spiritual ways of expression. In 1158, at the age of sixty, she began writing her second visionary work, *The Book of Life's Merits*. It took half as long to complete as *Scivias*, and was finished in 1163. Its central image is that of a giant man reaching from ocean to sky; he looks the world over and interprets what he sees and hears.

The penitential themes of *The Book of Life's Merits* may reflect Hildegard's frustration with the eighteen-year schism between the Church and the Emperor that began the same year that she started work on her second major theological manuscript, as well as the ugly human difficulties that she encountered with the Disibodenberg monks and with her own nuns when she moved her community to Rupertsberg. Meeting with adamant opposition on all sides, she may have found that this rupture focused her attention on humanity's grotesque vices and on God's remedy, repentance.

During this period, Hildegard also wrote an encyclopedia, the *Nine Books on the Subtleties of Different Kinds of Creatures*. It includes herbal remedies, other medical and mineral lore, and a bestiary, in nine books: on plants, elements, trees, stones, fish, birds, animals, reptiles, and metals. Hildegard followed this compendium with a healer's handbook titled *Causes and Cures*. Like many monastics,

Hildegard must have practiced medicine informally, on an as-needed basis. These two singularly nonvisionary works demonstrate Hildegard's inordinate interest in the natural world around her and her desire to learn all she could about God's creation in order to heal her fellow human beings and help them, and herself, live a healthy life.

Never one to merely sit and write, Hildegard turned to a new venture when she finished work on her natural history and medical works. Despite persistent ill health (such as exhaustion, fevers, and breathing difficulties), in 1158 she launched a series of unprecedented preaching tours. She traveled by ship, by horseback, and on foot, and, for someone not in the best of health, these long trips would have been arduous. The map at the beginning of this reader shows the rather impressive extent of her travels. The first tour took her down the Main River, from Mainz east to Bamberg, stopping at Wertheim, Würzburg, Kitzingen, and Ebrach, and preaching at many monastic communities.

On her second tour in 1160, Hildegard traveled west and south along the Rhine River from Trier to Metz, with a trip to the monastic community at Krauftal. At Trier she preached in public, a most unusual venue for a woman of her day, and she delivered her sermon on Pentecost, which was an especially appropriate ecclesiastical season for the fiery, light-filled visions of her sermon. Hildegard began it with her usual humble apology for being "a feeble little body lacking health, energy, a bold spirit, and learning," then added that "the mystical Light" had told her to chide the Trier prelates for shirking their duties and not blowing "the trumpet of justice," a negligence on their part that, she said, darkened earth's bright dawns and turned virtue's compassion into the coldest bitterness.[8] Hildegard's sermon would have been high drama for a medieval audience.

On her third tour, probably begun the next year, Hildegard traveled for a second time along the Rhine River, this time north. She went from Boppard up to Werden, stopping at Andernach, Siegburg, and Cologne. At Cologne, as at Trier, she preached thundering apocalyptic sermons to both clergy and laypeople. Her preaching in monasteries, churches, and public venues such as village marketplaces was a first for a woman of the Christian church.

Not long after her third preaching tour, Hildegard began her third and last major theological work, *The Book of Divine Works*, in 1163. Like *Scivias*, it took her ten years to finish. As she was finishing *The Book of Divine Works*, grief entered Hildegard's life when Volmar, her friend, confidant, and secretary died in 1173. In the Acknowledgments section of this, her final work, Hildegard reveals that when he died, her world was shaken. They had known each other for over sixty years.

While working on *The Book of Divine Works*, Hildegard was not idle in other ways. She also composed more music and letters, like the one she wrote in 1164 to the German Emperor, telling him how much she disapproved of his appointment of Anti-pope Paschal III. She also wrote minor works, including the *Vita Sancti Disibodi* (*Life of Saint Disibod*) and the *Vita Sancti Ruperti* (*Life of St. Rupert*).

During this already productive period, Hildegard also founded her second convent, some fifteen years after starting her first Benedictine community. The thriving Rupertsberg convent had become full-to-overflowing with young women dedicating themselves to the Church; therefore, in 1165, Hildegard bought the former double monastery of Eibingen, high above the town of Rüdesheim, east from Bingen, and across the river. Today on the site of this Eibingen convent stands St. Hildegard's Abbey, built between 1900 and 1904.

Hildegard would experience more precarious health from 1167–70, but nothing could keep her from her Benedictine mission. She began her fourth and final preaching tour in 1170, making her deepest journey south by traveling in Swabia, known today as Bavaria.

She rode or walked from the cloister Alzey to Maulbronn, Hirsau, Kirchheim, and Zwiefalten. The travel must have been strenuous. That same year she performed an exorcism for the highborn Cologne woman Sigewize and then accepted her into her community.

The Migraine Sufferer?

All of this activity would make anyone tired, especially a woman of the Middle Ages who lived before the era of MRI's, CT scans, and antibiotics. With all that Hildegard accomplished in her eight decades—the arduous preaching tours, the multiple well-received manuscripts, the founding of monasteries, the successful management of her communities, the personal care given to their more than one hundred monastic members, and her work as apothecary, dietician, naturalist, exorcist, musician, poet, letter-writer, and composer—it is hard to believe that she was so often sick. But Hildegard was frequently quite literally stuck in bed, unable to move.

Her symptoms suggest that she suffered from severe migraines. Most likely these were ocular in nature, producing auras that doctors today call "scintillating scotomas," *scintillating* for "flashing sparks," and *scotoma* meaning "an area of no-vision." Such neurological disturbances often start with a shimmering spot of white light that spreads and becomes bright zigzags bordered by silver. Even in the twenty-first century, ocular migraines and migraines in general elude the best and brightest medical minds. We still know so little about how to treat these excruciatingly painful, mystifying maladies; how much more would such an illness have disturbed the psyche of an intelligent twelfth-century woman who had absolutely no real scientific point of reference for it?

Sometimes Hildegard's visions are simply explained as a by-product of this agonizing, hallucinatory, and often crippling medical condition.

Migraines may indeed have contributed to what Hildegard saw, but surely not every chronic migraine patient can be considered a prophet. Hildegard seems a master at turning her weaknesses into strengths. Although these migraines and their paralyzing after-effects must have slowed her down some, they never physically impeded her work for long, and she never wavered from her dedication to God's calling.

To have such stamina in the middle of illness, diverse responsibilities, and profound artistic accomplishment, Hildegard must have found a way to tap into the well of holy joy. She defines *joy* as an awareness of God's secrets. But how can we be "conscious" of divine secrets? Hildegard tackles this age-old question head-on: *Can we see God?*

Her answer is synonymous with Psalm 19, that we can see God's vigor in the world around us:

> The heavens are telling the glory of God;
> and the firmament proclaims his handiwork.
> Day to day pours forth speech,
> and night to night declares knowledge.
> There is no speech, nor are there words;
> their voice is not heard;
> yet their voice goes out through all the earth,
> and their words to the end of the world.

Hildegard called this vigor *viriditas*, the "green" energy of agape love pulsing through the entire universe. Over and over in her writings, she chooses *viriditas* to express God's vitality and the ways His goodness and love charge the whole world with life, beauty, and renewal—literally, with "greenness." Her unique, creative use of this Latin word makes it something of a neologism in her work.

In Hildegard's mind, *viriditas* was first found in the green of the garden of Eden, but it is also the green of whatever twig you or I happen to be looking at in this present moment, whoever we are, wherever we may be. She knew that the natural opposite of this "greening" energy was spiritual desiccation (including what we often call "depression"). But, like God's mercy, His revitalizing *viriditas* has no limits. Wherever Hildegard looked, she saw that this "green" force animates every creature and plant on this planet with verdant divine love.

When I was a Senior Fulbright Lecturer in Seoul, winter seemed unending. I had no car and walked everywhere hunched-down and pulled-in for five long months of razor-sharp winds slicing icily through leafless trees in gray skies, until one day when I happened to look up, I was as shocked as I was thrilled to see that the dark, dust-covered bushes in front of Sogang University's Xavier Hall had begun unfurling the tiniest curls of tender green in the suddenly warm sunshine. That was good news! After an indefinite-seeming frozen time, nothing can be more exciting than spring. Hildegard lived through countless dramatic German winters and knew this knowledge, too, in her very bones.

I watched *viriditas* resurrect the Sogang campus that spring. It began glowing with the purest white cherry tree blossoms against bright green leaves. After the bitterest winter, they felt like a gift. This was also Hildegard's perspective. She saw flowers—literally the most beautiful reproductive form of natural plant growth—as the height of *viriditas*. To her, they symbolized in a mysterious way our obedience to God, and she saw God's crucified, incarnate Son as the best example of the Flower. In *Scivias*, Hildegard takes this notion further, using the image of a rejected flower to describe the fall of humanity. Failing to accept God's brilliant, sweet bloom, the first humans plunged humanity into a sterile darkness.

Hildegard's Benedictine Center

Another reason that Hildegard was able to persevere through her many potentially crippling difficulties was that balance was the most defining element of her life. Her ability to accomplish many things at once without losing calmness had its origination in the Benedictine center of her life. Before all else, Hildegard was a Benedictine abbess. As such, she was charged with teaching and taking care of her communities. Everything she did or said radiated from this Benedictine interior and its duties.

Hildegard's high regard for St. Benedict's *Rule* and its impact on her life are evident in her *Commentary* on it, a commentary that she included in a letter to a German monastic community that requested it. In it, Hildegard applauded St. Benedict's virtues, saying they made him shine "like the dawn," and she commended his *Rule* for being "neither too lax nor too strict."

As outlined in St. Benedict's *Rule*, Hildegard's structured monastic day included about eight hours for sleeping, some six hours each for working and meditative reading, and about four hours for the liturgical services. Her holistic creativity seems to have blossomed from her life's focus on the eight celebrations of the *Opus Dei* (*The Work of God*). The offices she regularly observed were Matins (at two AM in winter), followed by a short interval; Lauds; Prime (at sunrise); Terce, Sext, and None during the day; Vespers (at twilight); and Compline (at sunset). These were devoted to the repetition of the Psalter's 150 songs each week and to other prayers, reflecting the Benedictine principles of holy listening and humility.

Hildegard's life was an integration of prayer and work, just as St. Benedict teaches in his *Rule*, which opens with a call to listen and follow humble Christ:

Listen, Child of God, to your teacher's wisdom. Pay attention to what your heart hears. Make sure you accept and live out the directions of your loving Father. The work of obedience is how you will return to Christ when the carelessness of disobedience has taken you off the right path. My words are meant for you specifically, whoever and wherever you are, wanting to turn from your own self-will and join Christ, the Lord of all. Follow Him by wearing the strong, sacred shield of submission. Pray first before doing anything worthwhile, and never stop praying. Persist in it. God loves us as His children and forgives us, and so we must not grieve Him by rejecting His love and doing evil. We should always make the best use of the good things God gives us.[9]

St. Benedict's *Rule* also stresses the holiness of practical, ordinary work. This work was the pastoral heart of Hildegard's ministry. She took care of people. She was never the ivory tower intellect. Two stories prove this. When Hildegard turned eighty in 1178, she found herself in conflict with the Mainz clergy over a once-wayward nobleman whom they judged to have died excommunicate but whom she considered pardoned and had consequently buried in consecrated ground at Rupertsberg. The Mainz clergy wanted him dug up and moved to less consecrated ground. Hildegard refused. She even pointedly resisted their demands by personally erasing all evidence of his burial so that no one from Mainz could disturb his eternal rest. She had eyewitnesses on her side. They corroborated her story of the nobleman's absolution, and she would not cave in, even to the threat of excommunication.

Her resistance upset the cathedral clergy, and they issued an interdict against Rupertsberg prohibiting Hildegard's community from celebrating mass and requiring them to chant the divine office in whispers only, not to sing it. Hildegard retorted, "You've silenced the most beautiful music on the Rhine." But she never budged in her compassion, and the following March, Archbishop Christian of Mainz lifted the ban.

This conflict occupied much of Hildegard's energy at the very end of her life, but we must be grateful, in some sense, that it happened, because the quarrel, as obtuse and bureaucratic as it seems today, made Hildegard write down her fullest statement describing what music means to her. For the text of this hauntingly beautiful statement, see "To the Prelates at Mainz," in the "Letters" section of this reader.

The other story shows that Hildegard saw herself as a hands-on abbess. Everything else she did—even her art—was secondary to this vocation. When she founded her second convent at Eibingen, Hildegard was no longer a young woman and could have been excused if she had chosen to turn its leadership over to someone else, but she did not believe in delegating listening and caring. The greatest testimony to the loving nature of Hildegard's ministry is the way she managed this new convent. From its founding in 1165, the almost seventy-year-old abbess crossed the Rhine twice a week to visit those in her care there at Eibingen. She would make these trips for fourteen years, until her death in 1179 at the age of eighty-one.

–1–

Songs

I ask your help in the name of the peaceful Father,
His miraculous Word, and His truthful Spirit.
The awesome Father sent His sweet Word—
bursting with Life—into the Virgin's womb,
where He took on flesh, absorbing it like honey.
—Hildegard, from her letter to St. Bernard of Clairvaux
(1146 or 1147)

INTRODUCTION TO THE SONGS

ILDEGARD'S MUSIC IS THE MOST INTIMATE GLIMPSE she left us of her heart. It is passionate, fresh, inventive, bold, and layered with meaning. In her remarkable marriage of original sound and words sung at Mass and during the Divine Office, we recognize the truth that a great artist often succeeds by taking an orthodox subject and expressing it in a singular voice. Because of their soaring melodies and uplifting lyrics, you might think that these songs were written during an especially carefree time in Hildegard's life, but there were no such periods for this nun. She lived from illness to illness, conflict to conflict, responsibility to responsibility, and perhaps that is why we feel close to her, because, despite Hildegard's many accomplishments, her life was clearly filled with the daily grind we all experience; and she sang through it, and shows us we can, too.

Hildegard's creativity in music most likely benefited from a lack of formal training. Belonging to no school, and not influenced by a mentor, she took as inspiration none other than the living God who sent her visions. Perhaps because of this, the best adjective to describe her songs is *exuberant*, from a combination of *ex-* and *uber*, literally meaning thoroughly fruitful, abundant, or luxurious in growth. Considering Hildegard's predilection for and even love of nature images, this is especially fitting. Her songs are exuberant in their originality; they take the standard plainchant to new places, and her lyrical voice is intense, with dramatic leaps of up to two-and-a-half octaves.

In her position as abbess, Hildegard had a perfect environment for expressing her musical talents. She had a trained choir always ready to perform her work during the some four hours a day of liturgical chanting, and she had her very own scriptorium that could preserve her music. By 1155, a version existed of Hildegard's *Symphonia armonie celestium revelationum*, or *The Beautiful Music of Divine Revelations*, a collection of over seventy liturgical songs.

Over half of Hildegard's *Symphonia* songs are antiphons, musical dialogues taking place between two choirs and sung before and after every psalm of the *Opus Dei*. These are often the most lyrical songs, and they are the ones that will remind a modern audience of the pulsating, rich free verse of a contemporary poet like Rachel Srubas, whose *Oblation*[10] offers free verse meditations on St. Benedict's *Rule*, or of T. S. Eliot's *Four Quartets* and its orphic, meditation-influenced poetry. Nearly a third of Hildegard's compositions are responsories, normally more elaborate than antiphons and sung by a soloist alternating with a choir, after the lection. Hildegard also wrote fourteen polished longer works called sequences, which are more like lengthy prosaic hymns.

My approach to translating these Latin masterpieces has been to treat them all with a Hildegardian daring that represents their collective soaring spirit. Therefore, instead of making them merely "accurate," and, in the process, possibly boring, I tried to take the songs that are truly poems in the Latin and make them poems in our language, or—in the case of Hildegard's more prosaic sequences and sometimes less poetically agile responsories—I tried to make them as near-poems in Modern English as I could. I did this because when you hear these antiphons, responsories, and sequences sung to Hildegard's music, they are all goosebump-giving lyrical. So, sans music on this black-and-white pedestrian page, I worked to make Hildegard's lyrics as songlike as possible.

That said, I must point out that in Hildegard's day poetry was not a stand-alone subject as it is today. The foundation of the medieval curriculum was the *trivium* of grammar, rhetoric, and logic, and any discussion of poetry—what we call literary criticism today—would have been grouped under the arch-subject of grammar, while the analysis of a poem's similes, metaphors, and other figures of speech would have happened in rhetoric class. Poetry was also found under the rubric of music, located in the medieval curriculum under the *quadrivium*, or secondary studies of arithmetic, geometry, astronomy, and music. You did not have "poetry class"; you studied and discussed poetry while studying grammar, rhetoric, and music.

I should also like to point out that I have on occasion altered certain characteristics of Hildegard's lyrics when I have felt that they were wordy, uselessly repetitive, overly stated, frankly melodramatic, and unwieldy. I toned down her too-exuberant passages to spare the reader, presenting instead the soaring essence of Hildegard's songs. That means, for example, that I cut all of her resounding, introductory, and otherwise liberally sprinkled throughout "O's," as in the sequence to St. Rupert, titled here, "In Praise of St. Rupert," where Hildegard punctuates an otherwise satisfying hymn with phrases like "O Rupert!" and later, "O tender wildflower."

I have, on the other hand, tried to copy the strengths of Hildegard's style whenever possible. In her songs praising the Holy Spirit, I soaked the poems with verbs to emphasize Hildegard's own linguistic emphasis here, and I created line breaks that would focus attention on these dynamic verbs. These poems present her view of the Spirit as the Person of the Trinity who does and moves and soars and heals and makes all things happen. I have also tried to incorporate the many layers of meaning that explode from the excellent diction in these poems. For example, in the sequence, "In Praise of St. Ursula," Hildegard has the passionate future martyr say to Jesus:

> I want to marry you.
> Lead me along an unfamiliar path—
> let me be your bride—
> let me fly cloud-veiled
> across the clearest blue sky.
> And I'll race like sapphire to meet you.

In order to show the multiple levels of meaning that can be discerned at line four in "*per alienam viam ad te currens velut nubes que in purissimo aere currit similis saphiro,*" I had to add another word to my translation, because, while the Latin *nubes* does obviously mean cloud, a similar word, *nubo*, means to veil oneself when getting married. So, instead of having this devoted virgin Ursula simply say to Christ, "I'll fly like a cloud to you," I felt that she should say, "cloud-veiled," with the "-veiled" suggesting the union between this ardent virgin and God's only Son.

The titles that I chose for these twenty-seven pieces are my own and are meant to prepare the reader for a meditative reading of each poem. In "The Most Sanguine Moment," an antiphon on the crucifixion, the word *sanguine* in the title provides a meaningful play on words, because it can mean confident or cheerfully optimistic, but also bloody, from the Latin *sanguineus*. This word play is meant to focus our attention on the dual saving/happy and deadly/gory nature of the ultimate divine sacrifice. Also, in choosing the songs to include, I tried to represent Hildegard's musical corpus well by selecting mostly antiphons (fifteen), with a smattering of responsories (three) and sequences (three). The other six found here do not fit into neat categories of genre. Half of these are lyrics for which no accompanying music has ever been found, and they are included as the final three poems in this chapter. Hildegard's songs are presented here in the order that, as manuscripts suggest, she herself arranged them in *Symphonia*.[11]

Most of Hildegard's music honors the Virgin Mary and the saints, revealing how often and how deeply Hildegard and her community looked for inspiration and comfort to those-who-had-gone-before. The single largest category contains sixteen songs praising the Virgin's role in salvation. In one of this volume's poems praising Mary, "Grateful for the Unobtrusive Good," Hildegard's use of metaphors suggests that she saw no separation between symbol and fact. Metaphors *were* reality to her. Hildegard's point in this song is that the divinely made sun giving earth life is also, in a mystical way, the life-giving Son of God who as the Word made creation's every twig, including Mary, and yet was also Mary's "Bloom." In other words, God's Son is a sun is a Son is a sun, to rephrase Gertrude Stein.

In this song to Mary, the sun (also God's Spirit) shines on the Virgin Mary, the "greenest twig." She is a twig, not even a branch; but she is green with God's pregnant vitality, and her comparative insignificance (as a woman, and unmarried) prepares her for the greatness of God's Spirit to grow within her and produce the miraculous "flowering" of God's divine-human Son. Her weakness is her strength, a recurring theme in Hildegard.

Hildegard took special pleasure in writing liturgical music to celebrate the heroic lives of saints. Three of her favorites were St. Disibod, St. Rupert, and St. Ursula. St. Disibod was the seventh-century Irish bishop and hermit who founded the Disibodenberg monastery, while St. Rupert was said to be an eighth-century Rhineland prince. After a pilgrimage to Rome when he was fifteen, Rupert dedicated himself and his properties to God, only to die at the young age of twenty, at which time his mother honored his memory by founding a monastery on Mount Rupert. St. Rupert's Salzburg monastery was destroyed by Vikings in the late ninth century but today is one of the oldest active monasteries in Western Europe.

Hildegard also greatly admired St. Ursula and composed a memorable liturgical sequence about this legendary British princess who rejected a husband for God and was later martyred, tradition said, at Cologne, along with a group of 11,000 other women who chose Christ over earthly husbands. Ursula and the virgins were returning home from a pilgrimage to Rome when the Huns struck. Hildegard is well-known for her striking images, and the final metaphor of this song is perhaps one of her most unforgettable: The martyred virgins are pearls in a choker necklace meant for the Devil.

Songs

We transition now into Hildegard's celestial songs with a bridge that she herself used in her first major work of theology, *Scivias*, which concludes not with a vision, but with a concert in the thirteenth "vision" that Hildegard introduces by saying this:

> Looking at the clear sky, I heard many different kinds of music in it, expressing every meaning I'd ever heard in my visions. I listened to the happiness of those in heaven praising the Creator; I also heard them singing sad songs, telling those who'd forgotten God to praise Him; and I listened to the Virtues giving encouragement and advice. The singers made sweet music, like this.

Life-Altering Love

Endless Strength!
Your love authored life
when You spoke that one Word.
You're the One who ordered
order, created
Creation, Your own
way.

And Your Word dressed Himself
in flesh, embraced the disobedience-stained
form we inherited from Adam,
which is how He removed the sadness from His clothes.

The Savior's love liberates the world,
for what has ever been kinder than His incarnation?
His sinlessness breathed life into compassion,
cleaning that sad smudge from the boney outfit every human
wears.

Glory to the Father and the Son and the Holy Spirit!
He erased the anguish from our flesh.

Songs

To Sophia

You soar, sustain, and animate,
climb, dive, and sing
Your way through this world,
giving life to every beating
heart.

You never end.
       You keep circling, crossing over us
on three wings—
           one speeds through heaven,
           one holds the earth together with a kiss as light as dew,
           and one whooshes over, under, and through our lives.
We praise You, Wisdom!

The Sheep, Listening

Shepherd of our souls, and First Voice
of creation, now *let there be . . .*
freedom.
For we're still wretched creatures,
always weary, always weak,
and only You can rescue
us from the unhappiness
we make.

The Most Sanguine Moment

When the Creator actually spilled
His blood on the elements,
earth, air, water, and fire
screamed,
collapsed with grief,
shook from sadness.
Now, Father, with this gift
anoint our weaknesses.

A Prayer from Poverty to Greatness

Father,
we're so needy.
We beg You,
by Your Word
through whom
You made us rich
in everything we lack,
please (we're begging You)
help us, or we'll fail.
Don't let us darken Your name with shame.

Help us.

Songs

A Mystery of Mother and Maker

You sparkle like the brightest jewel
as the Father's sole Sun flows through You
like a fountain.
Through this Word, God articulated
the original matter He used to make this world,
which Eve disordered.

You're the mother of Light,
because He grew the Word in you
into a man—
using the matrix of your brightness
to speak the virtues into being,
just as the Word once used the original matter
to speak the world alive.

❧

The Open Invitation

The closed holy gate
opens today, to show us
the way to receive all
the serpent had locked up
in woman.
Come on through, now.
How?
In the garden over there, do you see
the Flower of Mary
shining in the dawn?

❧

That a King Would Bow

How miraculous—
that a king stoop
to enter the world
of the ordinary,
of the commoner,
of His subject,
of woman.
But God did this. Why?
Because humility,
ever the lowliest of the low,
always rises—
and triumphs—
over everything else.
And didn't that woman know the greatest happiness?
Cleaning up the ugly first mess,
in its place she set a beautiful bouquet:
the Flower from which the sweet perfume
of virtues flows.

And a Woman Would Stand Up

Hallelujah!
Your body enlightened all creation, Mary,
when your purity conquered death and you
became a twig of reconciliation
as that beautiful Flower blossomed from
your wonderful virginity.

Grateful for the Unobtrusive Good

Mary, whatever's small and unnoticed,
is like you . . . growing,
the greenest twig
stirring
in the rainy gusts that were all those questions
asked by those who lived before your time and
spent their lives looking for God's Son to come.

The sunshine warmed you,
and when the time was ripe,
you blossomed,
smelling like balsam,
and the fragrance of your Bloom
renewed the spices' dry perfume.

The earth rejoiced when your body grew
spelt.[12] The sky celebrated by giving
the grass dew, and the birds built
nests in your wheat, and the food
of the Eucharist was made for all humanity.
We feast on it, full of joy.

Kind lady, no wonder you're always happy.
Eve scorned these things,
but we praise our God on high!

The First Verb

The Holy Spirit animates
all, moves
all, roots
all, forgives
all, cleanses
all, erases
all
our past mistakes, and then
puts medicine on our wounds.
We praise this Spirit of incandescence
for awakening
and reawakening
all
creation.

The First Fire

Spirit of fire,
Paraclete, our Comforter,
You're the *Live* in *alive*,
the *Be* in every creature's *being*,
the *Breathe* in every breath on earth.

Holy Life-Giver,

Doctor of the desperate,
Healer of everyone broken past hope,
Medicine for all wounds,
Fire of love,
Joy of hearts,
fragrant Strength,
sparkling Fountain,
Protector,
Penetrator,
in You we contemplate
how God goes looking for those who are lost
and reconciles those who are at odds with Him.
Break our chains!

You bring people together.
You curl clouds, whirl winds,
send rain on rocks, sing in creeks,
and turn the lush earth green.
You teach those who listen,
breathing joy and wisdom into them.

We praise You for these gifts,
Light-giver,
Sound of joy,
Wonder of being alive,
Hope of every person,
and our strongest Good.

In Praise of Guardian Angels

Divine protectors, we praise your bright courage,
and celebrate archangels, who escort souls to heaven,
and thank virtues, powers, principalities, dominions, and thrones,
also cherubim and seraphim, who lock up God's secrets!
We praise you!

We praise your gazing
on the oldest love flowing
from the Fountain,
praise you for seeing
the Father's strength,
praise you for living, for
looking on His kind face.

In Gratitude for Perspicacious Men

Patriarchs and prophets,
you are men with spiritual eyes who walked hidden paths and saw
marvels,
stood in the transparent shadows and prophesied,
told us the living Light would bud on the branch
and bloom because it was rooted in brightness.

You saw the salvation of souls past, present, and future
coming.
Spinning wheels, you spoke
like mystics of the mountain touching Heaven.
Then He came.
The bright Light rose in your midst
and was baptized, consecrating all waters,
sent by the Father to reveal God's highest mysteries.

※

The Apostles as the Voice of God's Son

Spiritual warriors of Christ,
of the Rose that never grew a thorn,
your words circle the globe,
powered by God's Spirit, humbling
and besting those living in debauched indulgence.
As the Savior's family tree, you're rooted
deep in the Word's whole mission,
and when you accepted the Lamb's baptism,
going where He sent you,
you met men like beasts whose red hands
butchered their own best interests
when they attacked the One-Not-Made-With-Hands.

They still haven't found what they're looking for,
but you're the brightest light in the darkest night.

❧

The Mighty Wildness of Service

Offspring of the invincible Lion,
you lead by serving, Confessors.
Like angels, you praise God and help people.
Yes, you're conscientious in your service to the Lamb.

❧

In Praise of St. Disibod

Your soul was happy,
and even though your body was born of the very earth you
walked,
you disciplined the dust in yourself
during your pilgrimage in this world,
to live a fruitful life.
And, because you devoted yourself to contemplation,
you've been crowned with the divine
reason Who made you
His mirror.
The Holy Spirit made His home
in you, because you were crowned with the divine
reason Who made you
His mirror.
Glory be to God!

In Praise of St. Rupert

Royal, purple-bannered Jerusalem,
you're golden, your light,
unending. Your goodness
shines at dawn,
reflecting from your buildings,
and again at noon.

Rupert, your holy childhood shone, too,
in the red of Sunrise,
your youth blazing at noon,
your whole life sparkling like a gem,
impossible to hide,
though the foolish Vikings tried,
when they destroyed your shrine at Rupertsberg.
But can a valley ever hide a mountain?

Jerusalem, your sapphire-and-topaz windows
dazzle, and, Rupert, you shine among these—
we see the light of your enthusiasm,
in the same way that anyone in a valley below a mountain
can see your peaks covered even now in roses, lilies, and purple
aubretia.

Rupert, you're the tender wildflower,
the green freshness of the ripening pear,
the lightness of heart
those-who-are-never-mean know.
Your body was never tainted
by the song-and-dance of the ancient cave,
was never wounded by the old enemy.
Instead, the Holy Spirit made a symphony of your soul,
and now you sing in the heavenly choirs with the angels,
because you're Christlike in every way—
from your childhood on, you desired and respected God,
lived chastely, creating the fragrance of good deeds.

Jerusalem, the luminescent stones of your foundation
were once publicans and sinners,
but the Shepherd found them,
and they ran back to you.
Now they're in their place.
So your walls and towers shine with living gems
that soared like clouds to heaven,
powered by kindness.

We pray to you citizens of Jerusalem,
crowned and robed, and, Rupert, we ask you, too,
to help those of us who serve God
down here,
exiled.

At the Foundation of Goodness

Virgins are beautiful women
who look to God,
rise with the sun,
and build the things of peace.
How excellent you are!
The King noticed you,
saw Himself reflected there,
and made you His—
putting heaven's finest robes on you
and making you the perfume of goodness
in the greenest garden!

A Monastic Prayer for Purity

Best Friend and Lover,
help us stay virgin.
For we're dust
born to inherit Adam's shortsightedness,
craving the taste of the forbidden
fruit wherever we can find it, Savior.
It's so difficult not to.

Give us strength to follow You,
but have compassion on the hard way
we've chosen, trying to live a chaste life
as You did, King of angels.
We struggle, but still trust You
because we know You never stop looking
through the muck

for Your flowers and jewels.
Help us, then, Bridegroom, Confidant, and Redeemer.
Under Your red cross, each one of us promised
our hand to You in marriage, selecting You over all others
because You're gorgeous! Your fragrance fills us with desire,
and we long for You here in our exile.
When will we see You?
Live with You in heaven?
You fill our minds—
we hug You close
and wish You were beside us.

You are the invincible lion who broke open heaven
and came down to the Virgin in her royal chamber,
destroying Death and making golden community.
Let us live there with You, Sweetheart,
because You dragged us from the devil's greedy maw,
from the one who seduced our first parent.

In Praise of St. Ursula

Church, your eyes are sapphire blue,
and your ears Mount-Bethel holy,
your fragrant smell is a mountain of incense,
and your voice the music of cascading streams.

Faithful Ursula saw God's Son in a vision,
and she loved him, and she rejected a husband and the world,
looking directly into the sun instead,
and saying to that handsome young Man:
"I want to marry you.

Lead me along an unfamiliar path—
let me be your bride—
let me fly cloud-veiled
across the clearest blue sky.
And I'll race like sapphire to meet you."

When people heard Ursula praying,
they made fun of her.
Rumors started. People gossiped,
saying, "She's much too young
to know what she's talking about."
They only understood the truth after
Ursula's martyrdom, when her rejection of the world
was as visible as Mount Bethel,
and as fragrant as incense.

When the Devil entered-and-possessed the Hun soldiers
to massacre those noble women with her,
the four elements of this world—
earth, air, water, and fire—
witnessed it and mourned, crying
to God on His throne:
"Look!
The harmless lambs
are slaughtered
at their wedding!"

Hear them now and praise God's Lamb.
Sing to God!
For these pearls made from God's Word
wrapped round that ancient serpent's throat
and strangled him.

Three Antiphons for Church Dedications

Church, grieve your lost
children, because, Virgin, the snarling
wolf dragged them off—while they were standing
right beside you!
Let that cunning serpent meet disaster.
But our Savior's blood went looking
for your little ones.
Under the flag of the King,
He goes looking, ransoming
them with all His heart,
then asking you, *Ecclesia,*
to be His bride!

Sing for joy!
Mother, your children are found.
They're safe at home,
secure in heaven's harmony.
But you, ugly Serpent,
humiliated in defeat—
thought you held these children tight
in your greedy mouth,
but now they shine
in the blood of the Lamb.
We praise the highest King for that!
Hallelujah!

Willowy[13] *Ecclesia*,
wearing God's bright, bluer-than-the-purple-hyacinth
armor, you're the aroma of all people's
wounds.
Lady, you're the center of intelligence,
standing tall in the highest song,
anointed in heavenly music,
your beauty is a shining gem.
Hallelujah!

The First Daylight

You're the Word of our Father,
the light of the first sunrise,
God's omnipotent thought.
Before anything was made,
You saw it,
You designed it, and
You tucked Your all-seeing nature in the middle of Your sinew,
like a spinning wheel
with no beginning and no end,
still encircling everything.

Mary's Love Song

I love You, Son,
carrying You inside me
in the holy power of the forever-
turning wheel of the Trinity
who made me,
ordered my life,
shaped my limbs,
and placed You in my womb
to make all kinds of Music,
every sound a flower.
Today, a community of virgins
communes with me and You,
sweetest Son.
Help them.

The First Artist

Humans, God made you
in a profoundly sacred space
when the holy Divinity split
heaven open for the Trinity
to penetrate
and sparkle in earth's muck.
If you want to know why,
look at His humility and kindness.
Even the angels who serve God see Him in
us who merely walk on
land.

–2–

Scivias

(Know the Ways of the Lord)

> The most fascinating part of Hildegard's work is really her
> "cosmic theology," a vision of the universe that is both vast and minute,
> a dazzling view cast over the world.
> —Régine Pernoud, *Hildegard of Bingen:*
> *Inspired Conscience of the Twelfth Century* [14]

INTRODUCTION TO *SCIVIAS*

OW IS A MODERN READER supposed to read the visions of a medieval woman? The short answer is— with an eye to putting their spiritual truths into practice. Hildegard announces the purpose of her book immediately, opening *Scivias* with a bold command: "Look with me!" Shortly afterwards, she tells us why she wrote down her visions and what they were meant to accomplish—the divine Voice told her to articulate what she saw and heard in her visions, and for these reasons:

So now you must give others an intelligible account of what you see with your inner eye and what you hear with your inner ear. Your testimony will help them. As a result, others will learn how to know their Creator. They'll no longer refuse to adore God.

In other words, her visions are meant to teach us how to praise God and, from that praise, to love God's Son, ourselves, and others more, and also to trust the Holy Spirit for healing, forgiveness, and new life. Short for the Latin phrase *Scito vias Domini*, or "Know the Ways of the Lord," the *Scivias* manuscript is organized into three books, representing the medieval notion of perfection reflected in the Trinity. Book one has six visions, book two seven, and book three thirteen.

The twenty-six visions of Hildegard's first major book show that her way is always the way of embracing, not the *via negativa*. Her basic premise is Augustinian. She sees God as merciful, and she understands that creation is good, if fallen. But she improves on St. Augustine in her persistent, very diverse articulation of a glass-half-full, God-is-good theology.

Here in *Scivias*, Hildegard puts her startling, original visions to practical use in order to create an orthodox handbook for good Christian living. It is meant to teach followers how to live a loving, Christian lifestyle. While her visions may be stunning, Hildegard's theology is always well-grounded. It is in fact literally grounded, enough to make the sensitive reader think that perhaps Hildegard was also an avid gardener, for her images are often of planting and growing. One of the main themes of *Scivias* is the fertile virginity of Christ versus the sterile, unbridled sexual vices of the Antichrist. As we will see, Hildegard shows that all things grow in Christ and are fecund, but Satan is desiccation.

Book one of *Scivias* covers Creation and the Fall. Book two deals with redemption, describing salvation through Christ's incarnation and its presence in the contemporary world through the sacraments of the Church. Book three uses the image of a building to explore the history of salvation, reveals Hildegard's love of allegory in her focus on the Holy-Spirit-inspired Virtues, and presents holiness as a journey to God's kingdom. In its comprehensive treatment of Christian doctrine, Hildegard's *Scivias* resembles Hugh of St. Victor's *De sacramentis christianae fidei* (*On the Sacraments of the Christian Faith*), written just a few years before Hildegard started *Scivias*.

In Hildegard's day, *Scivias* was her most well-known work. Perhaps that fame resulted in part from the apocalyptic visions of its unforgettable conclusion. First the Antichrist rapes the allegorized female *Ecclesia* (the Church). Later, the Antichrist is sitting on top of a mountain of excrement, which signifies sin's disgusting nature, when a single, divinely sent lightning-bolt knocks this self-exulting imposter down dead.

In *Scivias*, Hildegard often refers to the terror of the Antichrist as approaching from "the North," by which she means Satan and the Antichrist. On a medieval map, north would normally have been on the "sinister" left-hand side, where our "west" is today, while "east" for Hildegard took the uppermost, "heavenly" position (our present-day "north"). This medieval "east" represented spiritual newness and the straight-up dawning of Christ's kingdom.

The final revelation of *Scivias* literally sings. It includes seven antiphons (a musical dialogue between two different choirs) and seven responsories (sung in "response" to a Scripture reading in church). Many of these honor the Virgin Mary. They are followed by an early, shorter version of Hildegard's *Ordo virtutum* (*The Play of the Virtues*).

A Blinding Vision

Look with me! In the forty-third year of my earthly journey, a vision from heaven filled me with such awe, it made me tremble. As I watched, out of its brightness a divine voice spoke to me:

How fragile you are, Human. Made of dust and grime. Articulate what you see and hear. Write it all down. Because you're frightened to speak out, and because your style is simple and unschooled, you must write down exactly what God shows and tells you, without relying on human rhetoric or intelligence. Let the will of Him who guides the universe, guide you in this work. Get to it. Speak of these visions.

This is what happened in the 1141st year of the incarnation of Jesus, Son of God, when I was forty-two years and seven months old. Something exploded like lightning from heaven in my mind, blinding me. It consumed my thoughts, warming my heart without burning it, as the sun's rays warm whatever they touch. All of a sudden, I understood what the Psalter meant, what the Gospelists wrote, and the meaning of all the other Old and New Testament books, even though my grammar was no good, since I lacked all formal instruction.

A Vision to Begin Writing

I've always had visions, even in childhood, but I kept silent. Later, I told these to only a very few in my monastic family. I've mostly kept them hidden until now, when God decided I should speak out.

I did not see these visions when I was asleep or dreaming, nor was I hallucinating. I didn't see them with my physical eyes, nor did I hear them with the ears on the sides of my face. They never came from simple seeing or hearing. No, I was fully awake, and I saw them with my mind. I heard them through my inner ears. This was God's will. It may be hard for you to understand, but it's true.

When I reached the age of accountability, a divine voice sang out to me:

> I am the living Light. I make the darkness day and have chosen you to see great wonders, though I've humbled you on earth. You're often depressed and timid, and you're very insecure. Because you're conscientious, you feel guilty, and chronic physical pain has thoroughly scarred you. But the deep mysteries of God have saturated you, too, as has humility. So now you must give others an intelligible account of what you see with your inner eye and what you hear with your inner ear. Your testimony will help them. As a result, others will learn how to know their Creator. They'll no longer refuse to adore God.

That voice made me—a heartbroken, fragile creature—begin to write, though my hand was shaking and I was traumatized by more illnesses than I could even begin to name. As I started this task, I looked to the living Light, asking, "But what I should write down?" and that Brightness commanded, "Be simple. Be pure. Write down what you see and hear!"

The Self-Doubting Visionary

Still, I didn't immediately follow this command. Self-doubt made me hesitate. I analyzed others' opinions of my decision and sifted through my own bad opinions of myself. Finally, one day I discovered I was so sick I couldn't get out of bed. Through this illness, God taught me to listen better. Then, when my good friends Richardis and Volmar urged me to write, I did. I started writing this book and received the strength to finish it, somehow, in ten years. These visions weren't fabricated by my own imagination, nor are they anyone else's. I saw these when I was in the heavenly places. They are God's mysteries. These are God's secrets.

I wrote them down because a heavenly voice kept saying to me, "See and speak! Hear and write!"

The Vision of an Iron Mountain

I saw a huge mountain shining like silver-white iron. On it sat the most glorious One, with a brilliance that struck me blind. On each side of Him, however, I could make out two subtle shadows in the shape of gigantic wings. In front of Him, at the base of the mountain, stood a figure covered in eyes. I looked hard, but because the figure had countless eyes, I couldn't make out a human form.

In front of this figure was a child in a tan tunic and white shoes. From the One on that iron mountain throne streamed a majesty that bathed the child's head, and this brightness kept me from looking directly into the child's face. Sparks flew from the Creator on the iron mountain, and these living bits of light flew beautifully around all of these forms. I also saw that the mountain had lots of small windows, and in these windows I could see the heads of a rainbow of people.

What does this mean? The huge mountain shining silver-white like iron represents the strength and eternal nature of God's kingdom. The blinding glory of God is the intensity of divine peace, which is beyond our comprehension. The wings made of a soft light that I could look on symbolize God's correction and punishment, which shield us from harm and help us stay true to Him. The eye-covered figure represents Respect for the Awe-Inspiring God, whose humility gives her the best vision. She doesn't have a human shape because her eyesight is too sharp not to bring God's otherworldly justice with it. The child standing before her symbolizes poverty of spirit.

The sparks I saw represent the powerful divine Virtues emanating from God. They love to embrace, enthrall, and protect everyone who respects God and loves poverty of spirit. The windows in that mountain show that we can't hide what we do from God. So don't be lazy. Solomon says, "A slack hand causes poverty, but the hand of the diligent makes rich."[15] Run in the way of Truth. Do good deeds that will count towards your salvation, and you'll gain the glorious, cascading Fountain.

To the person who has intelligence in the Holy Spirit and wings of faith—taste, embrace, and accept My warning in your soul.

Story of the Sinning Soul

Who am I? A pilgrim wandering in death's shadow. What path am I on? The wrong one. What comfort can I get? That given to pilgrims.

I know what I should have become. My body was designed as a sacred temple, a sanctuary shining with gems brighter than the sun and stars, because they radiate God's magnificence. The roof and the walls should have all been made of gems. The stairs would have been crystal, and the streets gold. I was made to be friends with the angels, because I'm a living breath God placed in mud. I was supposed to experience God. But no! When I saw I could focus on anything I wanted, my inmost self turned its attention to the sinister North.

I regret that so much now! For I was captured, robbed, blinded, and violated. My garment was torn. I was dragged to a gruesome place and subjected to the worst kind of slavery. My captors hit me and made me eat with pigs. They put me on the rack and tortured me. They threw me outside and stung me with scorpions.

Then they shouted at me, laughing, "Where's your honor now?"

The Soul's Repentance

I was afraid, and in great pain. *Where am I? How'd I get here? Who'll come to console me in my captivity? How can I escape? Can anyone stand to look at my wounds? Who'd want to be around me when I stink like this? What hands would dare doctor my injuries? Oh! Who'll look on me with compassion? My mother left me when I abandoned the narrow path of salvation. Who but God can help me now? What have I gotten myself into? Mother Zion, what's going to happen to me? I miss your mothering. I've missed you. You were so kind to me as a child. I miss the wonderful music I heard when I was with you. I must try really hard to escape by God's way.*

After I'd said this, I went down the narrow path and hid from the eyes of the North. I went into a tiny cave and wept because I'd lost my Mother Zion. I wept, too, for all my wounds. I wept for my sadness. I wept and wept. I cried so many tears, they absorbed my pain and bruises. Then I smelled something very sweet. It reminded me of my mother's soft breath on my cheek. That small comfort made me cry some more. I was so full of joy that I cried until it shook the mountain of my cave.

But my enemies heard me crying. They tracked me down and began shouting, "Where are you? You're our captive. We'll do with you as we like! Listen! She's praying to those living in heaven. We must do everything we can to keep her with us, or she'll escape. We must get her to follow us again."

Then I sneaked out of the cave and climbed high to a place where I thought they couldn't see me. They still came after me. When I saw a mountain looming in the distance, I despaired again—it looked so hard to climb: *I'm such a failure! What should I do?! I miss my mother's sweetness, but she abandoned me. I can't return to the North's painful captivity. Where can I turn?*

The memory of that sweet fragrance sustained me, however. It strengthened me and helped me keep going on that narrow path, heading East. But it was hard, because the path got narrower, and on each side, bushes of thorns and prickly thistles made my every step hard.

Then I saw poisonous snakes, scorpions, and other hideous reptiles slithering towards me. The snakes were hissing. I screamed, "Mother! Where are you?! Help me!"

I heard my mother say, "Run, daughter! The Omnipotent, Unconquerable Provider has given you wings. Fly! Fly over these things blocking your path!" And I did.

The Soul Recognizing the Body Sacred

Then I came to the sanctuary. It was built of durable steel. I went in and did good deeds. These bright works were totally unlike my former dark deeds. My enemies still attacked me with arrows, but I didn't notice until the gates of my bodily sanctuary were covered in sharp arrows. I had been that focused on making works of light. These arrows couldn't breach the building I was in. They couldn't hurt me.

So it was my turn to mock my enemies. I shouted at them:

The Builder who made this temple was much wiser than you, and stronger, too. Your arrows can't injure me anymore. At great cost to myself, I've fought you. You tried to kill me, but couldn't. The best armor and the keenest swords protect me. Retreat! You can't have me any longer.

The Devil's Tempting Mind Tricks

But then whirlwinds came, and I was afraid again: *How can I survive these, too? What happens when the Devil tempts me with his tricky words? He says things like—"How can a thing you can't see and can't do, how can it be good? Why abandon the things you know come easy to you?"*

The whirlwinds lie to me, too. I also hear many voices inside myself:

> *Who are you, and what do you think you're doing? Why fight these battles anymore? You know you're not happy. You're never even sure if what you do is good. Why let your mistakes bother you? Who'll save you? Where's your peace? Why are the things you like forbidden and the things that annoy you are what God's law requires of you? How do you even know these rules are true? You'd be better off dead!*

Acceptance of Self-Doubt

That's when I began to try righteousness. I found it a hard path to walk, though, for I started questioning myself again. I said, *This is useless.* I wanted to fly high, above the clouds. I dreamed dreams that were too big for me. I wanted to start things I couldn't possibly finish, and then I felt sad. When I attempted these things, I just got sadder. So the result was that I sat and did nothing. I was neither living on the hilltop of holiness nor in the valley of good deeds.

My self-doubt makes me miserable. I feel oppressed by all things. I grow desperate. Then I hear the Devil's voice, and my problems worsen. Terror panics me. I blame. I speak evil words. I afflict my body and soul. I abuse God's purity, healing, and greatness. I believe that everything good is evil and will injure me. This is a huge, unhappy struggle for me. It's a burden. I go from sorrow to sorrow. I'm so unhappy.

How does this happen? The old serpent is cunning and good at manipulation. He knows just what to say to make me choose stubbornness and error. I forget to respect God. I sin, saying, *Who's God? I don't know Him.* The Devil's poison arrow is the evil robbing me of my spiritual joy. I don't want to celebrate people or God. I doubt everything when I feel this way, including my salvation.

But when God helps me remember that He created me, then— even in the middle of my depression—I tell the Devil, "I won't give in to my fragile clay. I'll fight you!" How? When my inner self decides to rebel against God, I'll walk with wise patience over the marrow and blood of my body. I'll be the lion defending himself from a snake, roaring and knocking it back into its hole. I won't let myself give in to the Devil's arrows. I won't follow my lusts.

A Vision of Anger, Hatred, and Pride

When anger tries to burn up the temple of my body, I'll look to God's goodness, which anger never touched. I'll look to God whom anger never touched, and I'll become sweeter than the breeze whose gentleness moistens the earth. I'll look to the God of peace, because then I'll have spiritual joy as the virtues begin to show themselves in me, strengthening me with their vibrant greenness. I'll look to God whom anger never touched, and—because I look to Him—I'll experience God's calm goodness.

And when hatred tries to diminish who I am, I'll look to the kindness of God's Son and to His pain. How will I get myself in hand? I'll accept the thorns that give off the delicate fragrance of roses. They grew to honor the One who was faithful, and by controlling myself I'll bring honor to my Lord.

Finally, when pride tries to erect (on sand) a tower of emptiness in me, who'll come to help me? This is the old serpent. He wants to be higher and better than everyone else—always in the spotlight! He'd like to take me down with him. I'll cry out to God then, "Where are

You! I can do nothing good without You!"

I'll look to God who gave me life. I'll hurry to the holy Virgin who defeated the pride that crawled out of that ancient cave. Instead of building an inner tower of vanity, I'll become a sturdy, secure stone in God's foundation, because there's no way the greedy wolf who died on divinity's hook can beat me when I bow to humility and taste God's sweetest flavor. I'll stand inside His fragrance and resist all vices, protected by my own rejection of arrogance.

The Church as Loving Mother

"O that You were like a brother to me, who nursed at my mother's breast!"[16]

This is the Soul speaking. She also says, "Savior, because Your incarnation made You my brother, I get to suckle kindness and truth when I take the Eucharist." Anyone else who wants to can, too, because this nourishment is given to us by the divine Mother. The Virgin gave us life. She nurtures us with nature's abundance. Lord, the food of the Church is infused with Your grace. You give the Church the healthiest meals in the sacrament of your body and blood. You're the living Loaf. You're the pure Spring of living water. You're authentic. You give me Yourself, and in the Eucharist I kiss You, incarnate One.

The Lament of the Church

But then Mother Church cries:

I conceived—and do still conceive, and I bore—and do bear— many people who make me tired. They injure me, their mother, by getting into trouble. I mean heretics, and those who like to cause trouble wherever they go. These people have a penchant for fighting useless battles. They're bullies. They steal and kill and break their marriage vows and pervert the holiness of sex. They misbehave in other ways, too. They abuse me.

However, I know that many of my children change their ways. They genuinely repent and live eternally, while others let their stupid stubbornnesses take them to eternal death. My rebellious children reject my mothering. They ignore the comforts I want to give them. They turn down my delicious, nourishing food. They attack me. They break my heart.

But look after my lost children. Bring them back home to me.

A Passionate Flame

I've not got the sinew of a lion, because I've never been classically taught. I'm also nothing like an early Church Father, because I've never officially been a student. I'm merely a too-sensitive, frail rib with mystical lungs, who saw a living, blazing fire that couldn't be put out. I couldn't understand all I saw.

There was a passionate flame burning the color of sky, its light as gentle as breath. The flame was an intrinsic part of an unquenchable fire, the way a human's heart, brain, and lungs are part of each person, and, as I watched, this flame sparked and flared. Then the flame floated over a huge spherical darkness, and began knocking against it, striking blow after blow. Sparks flew. Heaven and earth were created from this, and they were brilliant.

Then that fire reached out to a small clump of mud and warmed it into flesh and blood, and when the flame breathed on this clod, it became human. The flame within the fire did this. The passionate, peacefully breathing flame then presented the human with a white flower. I saw that the flower was suspended in the flame the way dew hangs on the grass. The human smelled the flower's fragrance, but refused to taste it or touch it. That's how he rejected paradise and sank into a pitch-black darkness, and the human couldn't extricate himself as the darkness increased.

Three Enormous Stars Appeared

But three enormous stars appeared, then more celestial bodies of all sizes. All dazzled. Then the most radiant star of all rose and shone on the flame, as a light like dawn began sparkling on earth—the flame was drawn into this luminosity without being separated from the burning fire. This was a miracle, because in the brightness of that morning, God's Spirit rose.

For a time I saw nothing else. Instead, I contemplated what I'd already seen. Then I was told that the rest of this vision was a secret, for now. I heard a divine voice say, "You won't see more until a miracle of faith allows you to."

Then I saw a Man of Peace come walking out of this bright dawn. He emptied His light out into the darkness, and the darkness pushed back, until He bled. But when he released His blood and pale-white, dying skin, these hit the darkness so hard that the cold-to-the-touch person who lay prostrate in death felt the warmth of His finger, started shimmering, got up, and walked out.

You must know that the Man of Peace who walked out of the sunrise radiated more brightness than I can tell you. He kept walking until He came into His glory, where everything is illuminated by the light of love, and perfumed with His holiness.

This Light said to me:

Shame-filled, earth-shod woman—untaught and unlettered— remember you've been illuminated by My light. It ignites in you an inner sun, burning with divine mysteries and secrets. Don't be timid. Tell these. Although you're hesitant to speak out, don't be. Speak of the Fire this vision has shown you.

When the divine voice said again, "Write down what you see and hear," I answered Him:

But I feel dirty inside, dust of dust. I'm afraid. I'm a feather in the dark. Don't destroy me. I work exceedingly hard at writing down these visions, but I'm the least important person I know. I'm the lowest creature on earth. I'm so afraid. I'm not worthy to be called "human." Teach me what to say.

An Egg, a Chrysalis, the Eucharist

When the priest humbly speaks the genuine words of salvation over the Eucharist, its elements are metamorphosed into the body and blood of our Savior. How? In the same miraculous way that My Son took on human flesh in the womb of the Virgin, this oblation changes on the altar. It's a miracle. That's why this sacrament is seamless, the perfect union of the invisible and the visible, just as My only-begotten Son is the perfect combination of the divine and the human.

You've seen an egg crack open and a baby chicken appear, haven't you? You've watched a butterfly climb out of a cocoon, unfurl its wings, and fly away from its chrysalis, leaving it behind? In the Eucharistic offering, the bread and wine also undergo a transformation—into My Son's body and blood. This must be accepted by faith.

Humanity Fell into the Black Hole

Humanity fell into the black hole of betrayal and couldn't get up. It was lost. It couldn't help itself. At this point, I sent my Son to save the world. He's a miracle, because He is both God and man. What do I mean by this? He gets His divinity from Me and His humanity from His pure mother. Do you want to know what this means, too? First, think about the fragile, soft-skinned human body, then look at the stubborn and unyielding nature of your disbelief. Think how rocks are sanded and polished to be used in constructing a building—then remember how you refuse to be altered by your faith.

So listen. Anyone who owns a brilliant jewel takes it out of its box and has it set in a gold setting, so others can see it. This jewel is the Son of My heart, placed in the Virgin's womb, for the good of others. His sinlessness defeated death, and His mercy rescues all who love Him.

May the person with bright, alert eyes see this. May anyone listening with open ears understand. Welcome the Mystery with a kiss, and hug My words to you, because I am Life.

The Apocalyptic Vision of the Five Beasts

I saw five beasts in the North. One was a dog that glowed but didn't actually burn. I also saw a yellow lion, a pale horse, a black pig, and a gray wolf. They faced the worldly West, where I saw a hill with five peaks. Tied to the mouth of each beast was a rope that stretched from it to one of the hill's summits. Each rope was black, except the wolf's, which was half-black and half-white.

In the East I saw the young man I'd seen earlier. He was standing at the cornerstone, wearing a purple tunic, and this time I was able to see him from the waist down. Where his maleness was, he radiated light like the dawn. A harp lay across his body.

I also saw the woman I've seen many times before. She was standing as usual before the altar of God. I saw her from the waist down also, and where her femaleness was, she had eczema. I could see the black head of a monster there, too. It had fiery eyes, the ears of an ass, and the nose and mouth of a lion. This monster inside the woman opened its maw, then gnashed its hideous iron-silver teeth. From the monster's head, down to the woman's knees, she was bruised as if she'd been beaten. Below her knees, her legs were covered with blood.

Look! The deformed head pulled out of that place with such force that the woman shook all over from shock. A huge mound of defecation was stuck to that head. Then the head decided to lift itself up onto a mountain and climb towards heaven. Watch. An arm of divine lightning cracked down the sky and struck that head with such energy that it tumbled off the mountain, dead, and its spirit entered Hell.

Next, a horrible cloud descended on that mountain, smelling worse than anything you can imagine. It covered the entire mountain, and also that head. The people standing there were frightened out of their wits. When the fog didn't move, they panicked, screaming at each other:

> We're doomed! What is this? What was that? We're gonna die! Who'll help us? Who'll save us? We've been tricked and didn't know it till now! Omnipotent God, have mercy on us! Let us return to You. Take us back. Let us run to the promises of the Gospel of Christ. Ah! We've been so badly deceived!

See! Then that woman's feet shone brighter than the sun, and I heard the voice from heaven speak to me:

> Everything on earth is hurrying to its end. The world's troubles and its many disasters tell you this. But my Son's bride, the Church, will never ever be destroyed, no matter how many times she's assaulted. At the end of time she'll be stronger, more beautiful, more magnificent than ever before. She'll enjoy the sweet embraces of her Beloved. That's what the vision you just saw means.

The Five Beasts as Governments

The five beasts that you saw when you looked to the North represent five tumultuous, bloody periods of government on earth, in which we see how humanity follows the lusts of the flesh, and the pollution of sin will be a constant. We see humans attacking each other like beasts.

The dog symbolizes a time when people will be rude, but will think themselves fervent. They're all fired up, but they don't burn with God's redeeming honesty. The yellow lion is a period in which people start many wars, but this is a weak time and won't last, as the color yellow indicates. The pale horse is the epoch of sinful people, who submerge themselves in instant gratification, refusing to do anything good. This period will lose its sanguine strength and grow pale in its fear of failure; it will end broken-hearted. The black pig is a time when leaders wallow in the filth of immorality. The gray wolf is a period of plunder, when people are neither black nor white, but gray with deception.

These five beasts face the West because time is short, and these five periods will disappear as the sun sets. People are always rising and setting like the sun. As some are born, some die. The five peaks represent lust. The rope extending from the mouth of each beast to a summit represents how far people are willing to go to get what they want and how stubbornly they persist in their greedy pleasures.

But from the East comes the Sunrise of Justice, the Son of Man. He glows like the dawn, because His faithful followers endure in purity. The harp is a sign of the songs sung by the ones being perfected in their chosenness.

The Fate of Ecclesia *in the End Times*

The woman is *Ecclesia*, the Church. Her diseased female parts signify the lust, murder, rape, and greed that those who should love her inflict on her instead. Below the waist, where the woman is seen to be female, is a hideous, black head. That's the Antichrist, who seduces others into darkest evil. His lust runs amok. He makes people reject God. His avariciousness rips the Church wide open.

The woman's legs are covered in blood, because, as the world nears its end, the Church will meet with much violence. What does this mean? The Antichrist will thrive in his perverted doctrinal lies, and the Church will bleed.

Today, the Catholic faith dithers, on a global scale. The Gospel limps its way around the world. The early Church Fathers (who wrote so well) are ignored. People are apathetic. They refuse to read and taste the nourishment in the Scriptures. That's why I've chosen to speak through someone who is neither eloquent nor learned. I am the I Am, and I tell My secrets through her. I speak new mystical lessons. Through her, I knead clay and shape it as I wish.

Remember that I-who-created-the-ever-changing-world don't change. You know a gnat can't live if it flies into a flame. Similarly, a human couldn't live if he or she were to see My glorious divinity. That's why I only show Myself obscurely to humans. This is not unlike the way a painter reveals invisible truths to people through the images in his painting.

The Mountain of Excrement

Still, Human, if you love Me, I'll hug you to Me. I'll warm you with Holy-Spirit fire. When you think on Me, I'm with you. On the other hand, those who look away from Me, reject me, as I do them.

Arrogance made the Antichrist want to be number one. All who watched him grabbing beyond what he should were terrorized by the presumption of his insane pride, which is that mountain of excrement. The divine lightning blowing the Antichrist off that offal mountain is his own jealousy, always wanting more. No one will ever remember his beginning or his end. When people see that he's a silent, rotting corpse, they'll know he lied to them. They'll smell (and gag on) the error of their ways. But that woman's feet shine brighter than the sun, because many who went off the narrow path will return to My Son's Bride, and she will glow.

No mere human should ask, When will the world end? No one can know. Certainly no mortal can. It's the Father's secret alone. Our job as humans is to prepare for Doomsday.

Then I Looked to the East

Then I looked to the East and saw the One-who-shines-so-bright-that-I-can-never-see-Him-clearly, but I was able to see that up close to His breast, He was holding something that looked like a dirty lump, the size of a human heart, decorated around the edge with gems and pearls. This is our gentle Father hugging humanity to Himself. That's why no one can reject anyone—because the Son of the Father is God incarnate who Himself accepted the human form.

–3–

The Play of the Virtues

A human being is the work of God.
Because God made the soul eternal in nature,
when a person gives in to their lusts, they often regret it, saying,
"I stink like manure!"
That's because the soul has a natural inclination to hate sin.
—Hildegard, from an autobiographical section of her *Vita*

INTRODUCTION TO *THE PLAY OF THE VIRTUES*

IN THIS CHAPTER, we make a rather large shift from the songs and visions that we read in the first two sections, to Hildegard's symbolic drama, *The Play of the Virtues*, a splendid staging of the Soul's struggle with the Devil. It is also the earliest surviving morality play, and the only one whose author is known. Morality plays did not flourish until the fourteenth century, with *Everyman* as perhaps the best-known example. Hildegard was likely influenced by *Psychomachia* (*The Battle of Souls*), an early fifth-century Christian allegorical poem by the Roman Spanish poet

Prudentius. In *Psychomachia*, seven virtues help Faith when she is tempted by seven vices.

Hildegard's *Play of the Virtues* has a simple, dynamic structure. The prologue presents a chorus of law-abiding Old Testament patriarchs and prophets, rightly astonished to see the numinous New Testament Virtues. When the Devil enters in scene one, he starts seducing the Soul. This temptation is swiftly executed, and the fallen Soul exits, her sinning taking place discreetly off-stage during scene two. Hildegard crafted this prudent staging with the high-born religious sensibilities of her audience in mind.

In scene two, each Virtue explains who she is and what she contributes to the fight for the Soul's health. The Devil interrupts this chorus of Virtues to mock them. In scene three, the bedraggled Soul reappears, obviously traumatized but repentant. She converses with the Virtues, and the Devil is silent. In scene four, the Devil makes one last attempt to ensnare the Soul, but she resists, the Virtues tie the Devil up, and they all praise God for the victory. The final section presents mystical words from Jesus on the cross, sung as the Virtues walk triumphantly through the church, with the forgiven Soul marching at the back of their procession, in the place of honor.

The crux of Hildegard's play turns on clothing. If the soul could have realized and accepted that she is already "wearing" salvation, then she would not have succumbed to the devil's nudges. Hildegard is obviously thinking here of the undergarments God made for Adam and Eve soon after their fall from grace. She does not mean something we put on once a week (as we do on Sunday), but an indispensable article that we keep clean and wear daily, an integral part of our lives.

Knowledge-of-God does remind the soul that, as the "daughter of salvation" she is already wearing grace, but she brushes him off, saying instead:

I don't know what to do.
Where should I turn? I'm afraid,
and I'm uncomfortable in this dress.
I can't figure out how to finish my incomplete outfit.
In fact, I'd rather take it off and throw it away!

In *The Great Divorce*, C. S. Lewis's narrator describes clothing in a similar way. He says that heaven's citizens consider robes and crowns "as much one of the wearer's features as a lip or an eye," because "clothes in that country are not a disguise: the spiritual body lives along each thread and turns them into living organs."[17] The reader who traces Hildegard's use of clothing imagery throughout her writings is well rewarded.

Instead of the long-accepted title *The Play of the Virtues*, a more suitable moniker for Hildegard's *Ordo virtutum* might be the more literal translation *The Order of the Virtues*. *Ordo* means "a series, line, or row," literally, that "order" (or "obedience") that the Virtues (such as Humility, Charity, and Hope) bring to the world, and without them, Hildegard knew, only chaos results. She also chooses *ordo* for its useful military connotations of "rank and file," or a "line" of soldiers. It suggests the spiritual warfare the play depicts, and especially the seventeen Virtues as a mystical fighting unit. Additionally, *ordo* connotes hierarchy in many ways: It is the social "class" cherished by Hildegard as divinely determined, a community living under a religious rule, as in "the *Order* of St. Benedict" and "an *order* given by a superior," each suggesting the necessary obedience and respect for authority that is the *leitmotif* of Hildegard's redemption drama.

Hildegard's script lacks any sort of staging instructions, and when it is performed today, directors have wide latitude in blocking and other artistic decisions. In fact, modern translators number the scenes of Hildegard's play to more clearly portray the action, but in the original medieval play, such divisions were not there. I have followed the modern practice and have also added to my translation some descriptions of the virtues, taken from *Scivias*.

Hildegard mounted this piece by turning to her Rupertsberg nuns, casting some twenty females to sing the roles of the seventeen Virtues, the Soul, and the group of lamenting souls. Then Hildegard found a small chorus of males (perhaps from the nearby Mainz monastery) to sing at the beginning of the work as the chorus of prophets and patriarchs. She chose one male to flesh out the non-singing role of the Devil. (The Devil does not sing, because he has divorced himself from all heavenly harmony. He shouts his way through the work.) This diabolical part may have been voiced—or shouted—by Volmar, Hildegard's secretary.

The Play of the Virtues was likely composed for the May 1st, 1152 dedication of the Rupertsberg convent. In that case, the audience would have been made up of the aristocratic families of the Rupertsberg nuns, as well as the Mainz monks and Archbishop. The elite nature of the audience may very well have determined the exalted tone of this work.

The same year that Hildegard was finishing *Scivias*, her friend Richardis was asked to leave the Rupertsberg community and travel over 200 miles north to become the abbess of a convent at Bassum in Lower Saxony (near Bremen). Richardis's brother (Archbishop Hartwig of Bremen) had in fact ordered his sister reassigned there. When Richardis accepted the new post, Hildegard's deep fondness for her friend made her feel betrayed, and she tried to stop Richardis from leaving. She wrote Archbishop Hartwig and even Pope Eugenius.

It is difficult to tell how Richardis herself felt about this reassignment, but Hildegard seemed to think that her protégée's acceptance suggested that she was too concerned with advancement as a nun. Hildegard was ultimately unsuccessful in her efforts to keep her young friend by her side, and Richardis' departure from her community left Hildegard traumatized. The prophet and the mystic wrote her with rare unguarded words:

> Daughter, listen to me. I speak in the Spirit, overwhelmed by grief. It crushes the confidence and joy I once had in others. From now on, I'll always say: "It is better to take refuge in the LORD than to put confidence in princes."[18] I have to say it again—I despair, both as a mother and as a daughter. Why have you forsaken me? Why? You've orphaned me. I adored your goodness, your wisdom, your purity. I loved your soul and everything about you. I loved you so much, many people asked me, "What are you doing?"

The emotionally charged music of *The Play of the Virtues* may reflect this difficult time for Hildegard. As she was writing the musical allegory of the Soul's struggle with the world and loss of innocence, her best friend was literally leaving her, and she herself was bereft.

Once Richardis was settled in her new home in Bassum, Hildegard begged her friend to come back to Bingen for a short stay at least, and Richardis agreed. However, before Richardis could return for this visit, she contracted a fever and died. In time, Hildegard grew to accept the divine wisdom in events she had vehemently opposed. This episode in Hildegard's life shows her humanity and her ability to grow exceedingly attached to someone in her sphere.

Cast of Characters:

Patriarchs and Prophets (small chorus)

Souls Trapped in Bodies (small chorus)

The Soul

The Devil (the solo non-singing part)

The Virtues (in order of appearance):

> Knowledge-of-God
>
> Queen Humility
>
> Charity
>
> Respect-for-the-Awe-Inspiring-God
>
> Obedience
>
> Faith
>
> Hope
>
> Chastity
>
> Innocence
>
> Contempt-for-the-World
>
> Divine-Love
>
> Discipline
>
> Modesty
>
> Compassion
>
> Victory
>
> Discernment
>
> Patience

Here begins *The Play of the Virtues*

PROLOGUE

THE PATRIARCHS AND PROPHETS:
What are those? Clouds?

THE VIRTUES:
Ancient saints, why are you so astonished,
staring at us, awestruck?
God's Word was made obvious in the human form,
and that's why people radiate with us.
We edify every part of His excellent body.

THE PATRIARCHS AND PROPHETS:
On the tree of God's Word,
we're the roots and you're the branches;
you're also the apple of the living eye,
while we've been in His shadow.

SCENE 1
[The battle for the Soul begins.]

THE SOULS TRAPPED IN BODIES (complaining):
We don't belong here on earth.
What were we thinking when we strayed into sin?
We could've been the King's daughters,
but instead we fell under the influence of sin's darkness.
Living Sun, carry us on your back
back to the true inheritance we lost in Adam.
King of kings, we're fighting spiritually on Your side.

THE SOUL (naïve-but-happy, at first):
Loving Divinity, gentle Life
in which I'll wear bright clothes
(receiving all I lost after my first birth),
I pine for you, and call on all the Virtues.

THE VIRTUES:
Sweet creature, happy Soul,
God made you, shaping you
in His profound wisdom.
You love so much!

THE SOUL (happy):
I come to you willingly, full of joy,
I want the kiss your heart will give me.

THE VIRTUES:
Princess, we're obligated to fight with you.

THE SOUL (suddenly burdened and bad-tempered):
But I hate long working hours! I'm weary
of the tedious load I carry on earth.
I find it so hard to fight my humanness.

THE VIRTUES:
Soul, dear Friend, God's will created you.
Remember? You're made for happiness.
Why cry about something God already crushed
with the Virgin's help?
Through us, you can conquer the devil.

THE SOUL:

Help! Give me strength. Help me stand firm.

KNOWLEDGE-OF-GOD (to the Soul):

Stand strong, daughter of salvation.

Remember the grace you wear.

Don't lose heart, and you won't fall.

THE SOUL (unhappily):

I don't know what to do.

Where should I turn? I'm afraid,

and I'm uncomfortable in this dress.

I can't figure out how to finish my incomplete outfit.

In fact, I'd rather take it off and throw it away!

THE VIRTUES:

Miserable Soul, you have a sad conscience.

Why do you hide your face from your Maker?

KNOWLEDGE-OF-GOD:

God planted you here, and yet you don't know Him.

Why do you refuse to see or taste the One

who made you? Why do that?

THE SOUL:

God created the world. I'm not injuring Him.

I can hurt Omnipotence? Really? How?!

Besides, I'm just having a good time!

THE DEVIL (yelling at the soul):

Stupid, idiotic hard work—where has that ever gotten you?
Consider everything the world offers instead—look at it again,
carefully. It'll give you what you need. You'll even be famous!

THE VIRTUES:

What a horrible, obnoxious voice!
You harbinger of pain and sorrow.
But look! A miraculous victory
has already happened in the Soul's secret craving
for God, a divine longing full of sensual delight,
where (it's awful to have to say this)
just a moment before the will felt no guilt,
whatever it did, whatever its excess,
and this divine desire ran away then,
to escape the lechery of the will.
Innocence, mourn for this, grieve,
because you've never lost your integrity.
You've never been all-stomach
like a glutton. You don't know the craving
that devours like the old Serpent.

THE DEVIL (shouting):

Who's in control here? God? Don't tell me—you think He alone
is worthy? Follow me! If you do—if you do, I'll give you—and
everyone with you—everything! Let me tell you, Humility, you've
got nothing to offer your followers! Why, not even one of you
knows what you are!

QUEEN HUMILITY (She wears a gold crown crusted with
emeralds, rubies, and white pearls, and has
a radiant mirror on her breast in which the
image of God's Son appears.):
My friends know right well who they are,
we also know without a doubt
you're the old Dragon, the one who lusted
to fly above God on high, but
God threw you in the abyss instead.

THE VIRTUES:
While our home is up there
in those highest heights!

SCENE 2
[The Soul is not on stage in this scene.
Like the prodigal son, she has rebelled, left "home."]

HUMILITY:
I, Humility, Queen of the Virtues, have something to say.
Virtues, gather round. I'll strengthen you.
Then you can look for the lost coin,
find the drachma the Dragon stole,
crown the persevering Soul.

THE VIRTUES:
Most magnificent Queen,
kindest negotiator,
we come, dancing!

HUMILITY:
For this, delightful daughters,
I'll hold your place in the royal bridal chamber.

CHARITY (She is as blue as a fragrant, spring-
blooming hyacinth, and she also wears a deep
blue tunic with two floor-length gold bands sewn into it,
sparkling with gems, one in front and one in back.):
Virtues, I'm Charity, the flower of Love.
Come with me, and I'll lead you
into the shining light of the Flower
growing on the branch of the Virgin.

THE VIRTUES:
Sweetest flower, we rush to your side,
filled with deepest desire.

RESPECT-FOR-THE-AWE-INSPIRING-GOD
(She is the tallest Virtue, her nonhuman
body covered entirely with eyes.):
I'm Respect-for-the-Awe-Inspiring-God,
and I can prepare you, joyful daughters,
to look on the living God and not die.

THE VIRTUES:
Respect, you'll be most useful.
We devote ourselves completely to you.
We never want to be separated from you.

THE DEVIL (clapping sarcastically, then shouting):
Bravo! Well done! But—tell me now—where *is* this great
Respect—*where* is this amazing Love? Your champion is—*where*?
Your reward? Who'll give it to you, huh? You've not got the
foggiest clue what you're worshiping—you don't even know
whose favor you're trying to cultivate!

THE VIRTUES:
Look at you. You're scared stiff
of the most Honorable Judge,
and, for your puffed-up pride,
you were sent straight to Hell.

OBEDIENCE (She is fettered by snow-white chains
and handcuffs around her neck, hands, and feet.):
I'm lucid Obedience.
Come to me, beautiful daughters,
and my brilliant light will lead you home,
where the King will kiss you.

THE VIRTUES:
Obedience, you're the sweetest voice of all.
Listening to you is the right thing to do.
It makes us happy.

FAITH (She wears a red chain around her neck.):
I'm Faith, the mirror of life.
Cherished daughters, come to me.
I'll reveal the sparkling Fountain to you.

THE VIRTUES:

Peaceful mirror, we put our trust in you.
You'll help us reach that Fountain.

HOPE (She wears a light-colored tunic,
and her eyes are fixed on the image of the Cross
floating in front of her, her hands raised.):
I'm the sweet vision of the living eye,
the bud of life. No lazy trick deceives me,
and you, Darkness, can never dim my power.

THE VIRTUES:

Living Life, and comforting Friend,
you conquer Death's mortality.
Your observant eye opens heaven's door.

CHASTITY (She wears the brightest tunic of all,
which sparkles like a piece of crystal or like
the water reflecting the sun; a dove is over her head,
and looks ready to fly; her left hand is on her breast
and her right hand holds a royal scepter; and her womb
looks like a mirror in which a baby appears, the word
Innocence on this infant's forehead.):
Virginity, most excellent maiden,
how you linger in the royal bridal chamber,
burning in the King's sweet embraces
as the sun shines through you.
That's why your noble flower never wilts.

The Play of the Virtues

THE VIRTUES:

The flower in the field falls to the ground
in the gusting wind and pelting rain,
but you, Virginity, endure forever
in the symphonies of heaven's souls.
That's because you're the fragrant flower
that can never dry out.

INNOCENCE:

Flee, flock, from the Devil's filthiness!

THE VIRTUES:

Help us, and we will!

CONTEMPT-FOR-THE-WORLD:

I'm Contempt-for-the-World, a shining honesty about life.
What a miserable, foreign jaunt
this hardscrabble earthly existence is.
I renounce you!
Virtues, come climb with me up to the fountain of Life!

THE VIRTUES:

Glorious Lady, you always fight Christ's inner war.
You're so courageous! You trample the world
with your power, and win heaven.

DIVINE-LOVE:

I'm heaven's solid golden gate.
Anyone crossing through me
will never taste the Will's bitter stubbornness again.

THE VIRTUES:

Princess, you always find yourself enjoying
the divine caresses that the world runs from.
Your love for the supreme God is so tender!

DISCIPLINE:

I'm the one who lives simply.
I detest dishonorable things,
and am always looking to the King of kings,
embracing Him in highest honor.

THE VIRTUES:

Angelic Friend, you look so fine in your regal wedding dress!

MODESTY:

I erase, drive out, and trample on the Devil's smut.

THE VIRTUES:

You're helping build the heavenly Jerusalem.
You're blossoming among the white and shining lilies.

COMPASSION:

A person can become bitter,
because, when the heart holds resentment,
 few things can soften it.
But I'm determined to give a hand to anyone who needs it.

THE VIRTUES:

Praiseworthy Mother of all pilgrims,
you're always on the move somewhere,
forever anointing (and feeding) the poor and the weak.

The Play of the Virtues

VICTORY:

I'm Victory, I'm a fighter!
I hurl stones at the ancient Serpent!
I stomp on him!

THE VIRTUES:

Dearest Warrior, at the burning geyser that engulfed
the greedy Wolf, you're the glorious victor who was crowned.
We'll gladly help you fight that old Liar!

DISCERNMENT:

I'm Discernment, the light of life,
and the diplomat of all creatures.
I'm the unprejudiced nature of God,
but Adam's debauched choices drove me out.

THE VIRTUES:

Beautiful Mother, you're so sweet and kind.
You never injure anyone.

PATIENCE:

I'm the pillar nothing can weaken,
because my foundation is in God.

THE VIRTUES:

You're the One who stands firm in the hollowed-out rock.
You're the glorious warrior whose suffering holds the world
together.

HUMILITY:

Daughters of Jerusalem, God animated you under the Logos Tree.
That's why we remember how this Tree was planted,
and that's why we rejoice.

SCENE 3

[The Soul begins to find its way back to the Virtues.]

THE VIRTUES:

It's awful! We're left to weep and mourn,
because our Lord's sheep has run away from Life!

THE SOUL (sad and repentant, invoking the Virtues):

Divine Virtues, you're beautiful.
How majestic you are. You shine
marvelously in the highest Sun.
Your company is very sweet.
That's why—aargh!—I'm miserable,
because I ran away from you.

THE VIRTUES:

You're playing fugitive with God.
Come back. Come back to us.
God will adopt you as His own.

THE SOUL:

No! I'm too afraid.
I got carried away with the burning confection of lust,
and I have sinned. That's why I don't dare enter in.

The Play of the Virtues

THE VIRTUES:
Don't be afraid.
Don't run away.
The good Shepherd is searching for you.
You're His lost sheep.

THE SOUL:
Then you must help me, right now.
My wounds smell awful.
They fester where the ancient,
poisonous serpent bit me.

THE VIRTUES:
Hurry! Run to us!
Just retrace your steps.
With us as friends, and in our company,
you'll never lurch
or fall.
God will heal your every injury.

THE SOUL (penitent, to the Virtues):
I'm the sinner who ran from Life,
returned to you, sorely wounded.
Please hand me that shield of redemption you have.
Dearest Warriors of Queen Humility,
shining like white lilies and red roses,
yield to me, though I banished myself
from you and made myself a stranger.
Help me, so in the blood of God's Son
I can rise up, strong.

THE VIRTUES:

Fearful Soul, be brave. Hang tough.
Here, put on the armor of Light.

THE SOUL:

Help me, Humility.
You're the best medicine.
Watch my back.
Arrogance has broken me
and left me scarred.
Now I'm running to you, so rescue me!

HUMILITY:

Virtues, on account of Christ's wounds,
accept this sorrowful sinner, with all her scars.
Bring her to me.

THE VIRTUES:

We're here to take you Home.
We'll never abandon you.
You'll be celebrated by everyone in heaven.
We sing this symphony in your honor.
It's only right that we should sing!

HUMILITY:

Miserable daughter, let me hug you.
The great Physician was severely wounded
for you. He suffered bitterly.

The Play of the Virtues

THE VIRTUES (to Humility):
Living Spring, your kindness is tremendous.
You've never rejected anyone's friendship.
You didn't even reject those who rejected you.
Instead, you knew with keen foresight
how they could avoid the fate of the fallen angels
(who overestimated their own power,
because nothing in the law supports such greed).
That's why you can rejoice, Jerusalem, our daughter,
because God is returning to you those many people
whom the Serpent wanted to steal from you,
but now they shine even more brilliantly than they did before.

SCENE 4
[The Virtues defeat the Devil, and the Soul returns in peace to God.]

THE DEVIL (to the Soul):
Just who do you think you are—and where do you think you're
from? I had you in my power—you were *totally* in step with
me—I was leading you out. But now—no!—you're turning back.
You may have foiled me for the moment, but I won't give up
without a fight—I'll come after you, and when I catch you, you
can be sure I'll kill you!

THE SOUL (penitent):
I turned and ran away from you
once I realized I'd chosen the wrong path,
but now I say to you, you old Fraud,
bring it on!
Queen Humility, come here, please.
Help me with your medicine.

HUMILITY (to Victory):

Victory, you conquered this enemy in heaven.

Attack him like a warrior now.

All of you, tie the Devil up.

VICTORY (to the Virtues):

Come, strongest, bravest, most glorious Warriors.

Help me conquer this Fallacy-Maker!

THE VIRTUES:

Dearest Warrior, at the burning geyser that engulfed

the greedy Wolf, you're the glorious victor who was crowned.

We're happy to help you fight that old Liar!

HUMILITY:

Bright Virtues, bind the Enemy!

THE VIRTUES:

Dear Queen, whatever you wish, we do.

[Satan is bound up.]

VICTORY:

Allies, rejoice! The ancient Serpent is tied up.

THE VIRTUES:

We praise You, Christ, King of the angels!

CHASTITY:

God gave me the power to trample on your head,
when as a virgin I cultivated a sweet miracle,
and the Son of God came into the world.
That's why you've been evicted, Devil,
with all your loot. Now everyone in heaven rejoices,
because your greed has been defeated.

THE DEVIL (tied up, but still shouting):

You've no idea what you're talking about! You speak of "cultivat-
ing," but you've got no idea what that word means—After all, your
own womb's an empty vacuum, isn't it? *Isn't it?* Has it ever known
the sensuous, spectacular form a man can give it?—No! See how
wrong you are? You've completely ignored God's command to "be
fruitful and multiply." So what I'm saying is—Are you listening?—
You don't even want to find out *who you really are*!

CHASTITY:

Your words can't harm me.
How can they make me impure?
And, furthermore, I did give birth to a Man.
His nativity attracts all humanity to Himself,
and away from you.

THE VIRTUES:

God, who are You? All by Yourself
You vaporized the hellish brew
guzzled down by publicans and sinners,
who now shine in heavenly kindness.
That's why we're keen to praise you, King!

Omnipotent Father, from You
gushed a spring of fiery Love.
Lead Your children well.
Help them sail through life's waters,
with a good wind, so we can guide
them into the celestial Jerusalem.

PROCESSIONAL

THE VIRTUES AND THE SOULS:
When the world began,
everything pulsed with life
and was the tenderest shade of green.
Flowers blossomed everywhere.
But, after the Fall, everything green faded.
The Warrior-of-Truth saw it all and said:
> I see what happened, but my house is not yet full.
> Look at me instead.
> I'm the image of your Father.
> Know my broken body
> broken for you. I'm exhausted.
> I'm tired of being made a laughing-stock.
> It goes straight through me.
> Even my followers lose heart.
> But remember this.
> The original abundance of green
> did not have to shrivel up,
> and your faith will see its way to strength,
> until you know the divinity of my jewel-covered body
> intimately, a gem in each injury, and each injury a bud.
> Look, Father! See my wounds?

Now, let people everywhere kneel before God the Father,
who'll hand us strength on strength.

—4—

Selections from Her Letters

> She denounced the vices of society, of kings, nobles, bishops, and priests in unmeasured terms, but the Emperor, bishops, abbots, and laymen came to ask for her advice.
> —The Right Reverend Frederick G. Holweck,
> domestic prelate to Pope Pius XI,
> *A Biographical Dictionary of the Saints*[19]

INTRODUCTION TO THE LETTERS

ALTHOUGH MEDIEVAL LETTERS were not usually the personal communications we think of when we speak today of "letters" or even "e-mails," Hildegard's bright energy runs through hers, even when she is talking in her most prophetic voice. Eschewing salutations, Hildegard prefers to open her letters with the voice of God. She often begins, "The Living Spring says—" and she likes to close with this reminder (using the same divine voice): "This writing doesn't come from any human person, but from the living Light. May all who hear it see and believe in Me."

Also, although Hildegard keenly felt that it was her responsibility to turn the mystic language of her visions into something intelligible to others, her writing always trails clouds of glory, as Wordsworth might have said, because in it many voices blend. We see this quality in her letters, too. In addition to God ("the living Spring" and "the living Light"), we hear Humility, Chastity, and other virtues speak, and, interwoven with them, we hear Hildegard's own verve. The public nature of medieval letters sheds only a little light on the elusive quality of this Benedictine nun's personality, but her dynamic energy is never in question.

A splendid example of the nature imagery central to Hildegard's work is found in a letter she wrote responding to a polite-but-critical letter she had received from Mistress Tengswich, the superior of a foundation of canonesses in Andernach and the sister of Richard of Springiersbach. Tengswich and her brother were reformers; they advocated apostolic poverty, and Tengswich vehemently disagreed with some of Hildegard's approaches to monastic life. Her principal concern was that Hildegard permitted the virgins in her community to let their hair down for liturgical celebrations. Tengswich may have been referring to a costumed performance of *The Play of the Virtues*.

Hildegard's nuns did adorn themselves with white floor-length silk veils, golden rings, and gold-filigree crowns (with the figure of a Lamb on the front, and crosses on the back and sides). In these regal costumes, the celebrants would have looked stunning, and Hildegard approved. She must have enjoyed the splendid procession made by these poised noble women singing psalms.

Hildegard's response to Tengswich shows that in the hierarchy of Hildegard's mind, virgins were the apex of creation. Marriage was not "bad," but Hildegard taught that it was a consequence of the Fall and therefore could never be a calling as exalted as virginity. Her virgins were special to God because they were pure and because they were intimate with God's Son (who was and is and will be *Viriditas*); therefore her nuns were co-participants in God's rejuvenating Energy. The poet Dylan Thomas plants the word *green* throughout his work to suggest something equally mysterious: "The force that through the green fuse drives the flower / Drives my green age," he says, and in "Fern Hill," he chooses *green* seven poignant times to describe the root vitality of his childhood, when he was "happy as the grass was green."

But Mistress Tengswich played Grinch to Hildegard's idea of *viriditas*. Wearing a pinched beatific smile much uglier than honest seething, Tengswich objected to the extravagant way Hildegard dressed those in her care, backing her complaint with Paul's letter forbidding women to braid their hair, wear gold or pearls, or clothe themselves sumptuously.[20] Hildegard agreed with Tengswich that married women should dress modestly, but her letter to Tengswich shows that she vigorously defended her virgins as exempt from this stipulation.

Mistress Tengswich also objected to Hildegard's accepting only well-born, wealthy women into her community, rejecting those with less-exalted status in society and less money. Hildegard countered Tengswich's objection by demanding (in un-Benedictine fashion), "Who lumps together their different farm animals—cows, sheep, donkeys, and goats—all in one barn?" She reminded Tengswich that God establishes both the heavenly hierarchy of angels and the earthly one, and that she is only trying to be commonsensical in accepting into her community those who will get along with each other and not fight over who has more and who has less. To support her argument, Hildegard quoted Job 36:5: "Surely God is mighty and does not despise any; He is mighty in strength of understanding." She did concede that God does not love people for their status but for their kind deeds and humble hearts.

Other letters of particular interest included in this reader are these: Hildegard's letter to the Belgian monk Guibert, in which she describes with splendid detail the nature of her divine visions; Hildegard's many sometimes shockingly bold letters to royalty; her extremely long letter to Abbot Helengerus, also given by the abbess at Disibod as a sermon; her letter to Abbot Kuno in which she responds to his request for songs on St. Disibod by sending him several; her gentle letters to monks and nuns with spiritual questions; and her letter to the Prelates of Mainz, which contains one of the most sublime paragraphs ever written about the divine origin of music.

To Bertha of Sulzbach, First Wife and Empress of Byzantine Emperor Manuel I Comnenus, also Known as Empress Irene
(1146 or After)

Listen to what God's Spirit has to say to you. In winter, God lets the tree He loves hibernate, but in summer, He makes it bloom abundantly and protects it from every disease. This is you. Remember also that every polluted body of water is purified by the stream gushing from the rock in the East, a clean, fast-running river. Who is like this river? Those whom God grants success and honor. They're not ruled by the poisonous North wind and its advancing evil.

Turn to God. Be confident that He has touched you. Continue to give Him the burnt offerings of your heart's openness. Sigh, and know He hears you. He'll give you the child you wish for, and every joy you need. Yes, the Living Eye watches over you. He wants you to live eternally.

❦

To Mistress Tengswich (Between 1148–50)

The living Spring is speaking to you. The fire-breathing serpent blew danger into woman—lust. So she must live in her cell and be chaste. Why? The beauty of woman sparkled in the Ur-root, when she was given her womb, the inner cell that gives birth to every person. Why is woman so radiant? God's hand made her. He gave her an awesome beauty. Woman, what a marvelous creature you are! By grounding yourself in the Sun, you conquer the world.

Yes, the Apostle Paul does say a married woman ought to be modest in dress and manner, because she belongs to her husband. In this modesty, she is also following the law of the Creator, who warned the devil: "Therefore what God has joined together, let no one separate."[21] But listen to Me. The earth's clouds, oceans, rivers, dew, and streams soak everything, keeping the grass (and all else) green, until winter comes, destroying the flower's beauty. Everything disappears then for a season, earth's energy hidden. Likewise, a married woman must be modest, not given to showy dress.

But these rules don't apply to virgins, because they're the green of an eternal Springtime. They're the closest thing we have to Eden. A virgin wears her hair long, covering it up only out of humility, to protect herself from pride's sharp claws. Virgins in their purity are married by the Spirit to holiness, and this bond gives them the freedom to present themselves to God as gifts. Virginity is also the brightest dawn, so virgins wear white robes, symbolizing their brilliant engagement to God's Son. They promise to be one with Him in body and mind forever.

Remember God has given each one of us common sense so we won't ruin our good names. For example, why would anyone put their shoulder against a mountain they can't possibly shift? Why not live in the valley instead and learn day-by-day who you are? Why not stay there and explore your potential and how you can best express it?

These words don't come from a human being, but from the living Light. Let those who hear, see and believe where these words really came from.

To the Abbot of Busendorf (About 1150)

The living Light says to you—Serve Me well, even in your mind. Watch yourself. Be disciplined. Fly like the eagle, always looking sunward. Throw all of your energy into this, and never gravitate to the shadow. Don't let yourself peer around corners with idle curiosity. Instead, persist in doing good. Keep your hand to the plow. Focus on God, and He'll help you tend your flock.

If you keep your eyes on the Light, ennui and exhaustion can't defeat you. So reject sin's darkness—God wants your good deeds to be pure and selfless. He wants you not to pay any attention whatsoever to the world's petty concerns. May you live forever.

A Second Letter to the Abbot of Busendorf (About 1150)

Visions often illuminate my soul when I'm completely awake. In one of these, I saw a whirlwind in your monastery. It was really a hurricane, and its lightning and churning black clouds shook the very foundation of your community.

I also saw the three colors of your soul. It is black with hatred and anger, and gray with the smoke of perverse hungers. The third color, however, is the dawn-red of goodness that starts in the godly sorrow of repentance. Then I watched a wondrous light rising up to God from some of the members of your congregation. For these faithful few, God supports your entire community with His grace.

Excellent shepherd, look at the field God has blessed with a good harvest. See the dark cloud heading towards this field? It will destroy all the fruit. This storm is the indolent, spiteful heart of someone who knows what good needs to be done and can make it happen, but who chooses to be lazy and to give in to hatred, instead of doing good works.

Son of God, run from these tendencies in yourself. Let the fire of the Holy Spirit inspire you to work in the field and harvest its fruit. For the day comes when you'll no longer be able to work.

❧

To the Margravine Richardis of Stade, Mother of Richardis, Hildegard's Dearest Friend, and Grandmother of Adelheid
(1151)

I beg you—don't upset my soul so much that you make me cry angry tears. I beg you. Don't cut me to the quick. Don't wound me deeply over my most-loved daughters, Richardis and Adelheid.[22] Even now I see them in my mind, wearing pearls made of virtues and radiant at dawn. Don't make yourself responsible for the loss of their honor. Beware of this.

You shouldn't recommend them for the positions of abbess. That is absolutely, absolutely, *absolutely* not God's will. Nor is it good for the salvation of their souls. You're their mother. You mustn't spoil them spiritually. Later you'll only be left to mourn. May God show you what to do and strengthen your resolve to do it. Remember, our time here is short.

To King Frederick, Later Emperor Barbarossa (1152)

You must remember that humanity needs earthly rulers like you, King. So listen. A man standing on a tall mountain surveyed the valleys below him, watching what people were doing. The rod of correction in his hand made wilted things grow and sleeping people wake up. Because he was wise, he also knew when to be lenient.

However, when this man wasn't paying attention, a stormy cloud blew in and filled those valleys, and black crows and other birds tormented the people who lived there. King, pay attention. Your kingdom is overrun by mendacious factions. Their dark sins cloud your dominion. Greedy, they trash the Lord's territory. With the rod of mercy, King, rule over the lazy and the licentious.

You've got much to live up to in your name, King of Israel. God will judge you later, and you don't want to be ashamed. God forbid! Lawgivers must model themselves after those who came before them and ruled honestly, and they must reject the bad example set by loafing prelates who indulged their dirty lusts. Run from them, King. Be a brave knight instead. Put on your armor and fight the devil, or God will destroy you. You don't want to be shamed before your whole kingdom.

May God release you from eternal damnation. May your leadership be a time of new growth, not a time of shriveled expectations. Reject greed. Live moderately. The omnipotent King loves self-discipline. May God defend you, and may you live eternally.

A Second Letter to King Frederick (1152 or Later)

King! Think before you act. You must learn to do this. I saw you in a spiritual vision, and, before the Living Eye, you looked like either a foolish little boy or a totally insane man. But you still have time to be a ruler. This is your warning.

Be careful, or the omnipotent King will destroy you for your blindness. You'll be punished for how your eyes refuse to see that you must hold the rod of correction correctly. You're not ruling right. Don't act in ways that renounce God's grace.

To Duke Welf VI of Altdorf, Also Known as Duke Guelf VI (1153)

Listen to the Living Eye. God made you a prince in this world, and you're lucky to have this divine legacy, because it means you won't be rejected by God or by the world. So why are you rejecting God's invitation? You do this when you choose immorality. Why do you spend your days bragging, stuffing yourself like a glutton, and getting drunk?

A deep darkness also envelops you because you've wronged your marriage. God wants your union to be one, as the body and soul are one. If you don't conquer this fault of yours, you'll be held in contempt by the living Light, and you'll never have a son.

May God wake you up and make you stop giving in to getting drunk. Then He'll help you live happily for all eternity.

To Pope Anastasius IV (1153 or 1154)

Bright defender and consummate leader of God's holy city! Listen to the One who lives forever and never wearies. Your wisdom weakens. You're tired, and the people around you are arrogant. Pull up these evil roots, who strangle the flowers and other good plants. You've turned your back on justice, who is God's daughter. She was yours to protect, but you've merely stood by and watched her thrown to the ground by violent men, who trample her clothing and crown.

When these immature hypocrites call for "Peace!" their words are meaningless, like the din of barking dogs, and when they mouth platitudes (while they seethe inside), their attempt at harmony is nothing but a foul noise, like the stupid cackling of hens. They lie. They secretly want to bite someone—they're like the dog that wags its tail before it sinks its teeth into a faithful knight. Why haven't you corrected them? They're blind and foolish. They love chaos. You're supposed to fight evil!

Don't forget that whatever God made, radiates. So listen. Before God made the world, He said to Himself, "Here's My dear Son!" and from this original Word, the world was formed. Then God said, "Be!" and all kinds of animals appeared. Our God creates, but evil is never creative. It's nothing, merely the by-product of rebellion. Through His Son, God saved humanity, clearly rejecting immorality—stealing, stubbornness, murder, hypocrisy, and bullies.

That's why you as pope must never collude with corruption. If you do, you confuse those who look to you as their leader, because, in effect, you're saying to them, "Embrace what's really nothing." You must be a mature leader. You must look to the mountains, to the community of clergy all around you, to strengthen your faith. If you humble yourself, they'll lift you up.

Listen to the eternal One. Today many people have chosen to walk a lust-riddled path that leads straight to sadness. But healing comes from within. Then you'll know abundant joy and the dawning of a fresh and abiding enthusiasm. You'll realize anew how precious-beyond-words life is.

May you, Father and Shepherd, find the path of justice, because you don't want to be reprimanded by the great Physician for not disciplining your sheep. Remember that—through penance—any thoughtless act can be cleansed. Get back on the right path. God will guide you. He'll lead you back into His flock, where you'll feel His eternal blessing.

❧

To the Countess Oda of Eberstein (1153 or 1154)

The abundant Light says this—Hear Me, human. Once upon a time, there was a valley that was sometimes as dry as a desert, and was sometimes as gorgeous as a blooming garden. But it could never be counted on to grow well, and, even though it was sometimes beautiful to look at, it was not very useful in growing nourishing plants.

This is your mind. Sometimes you look inside yourself and see the weakness of your conscience—that's when you dry up like a desert, because you despair. Later, however, your mind rouses itself and soars, as fragrant as the mountain of myrrh and incense, when you struggle with yourself, which brings you back to life and makes you grow.

How you vacillate. One moment you're praying, "I'm sorry for my sins." But later you shrivel up in your own self-indulgent will. You rush after possessions and forget to do good works, neglecting to exercise your spiritual muscles. Your heart sighs, saying, "I so want to do good works," but the longing remains a mere thought. The act

105

never sees the light of day. That's why you wilt in your sins. Yes, turn to God, but in good works. Then He will accept you.

Listen. Notice that your heart withers when you do evil, but grows lush and green when you do good. Submit to God by recognizing His presence in your good actions. Anyone who does good sees God. But the person who only *thinks* about doing good works is like a mirror that reflects an image, though nothing and no one are standing in front of that mirror. Get up and get going, then.

You may argue—"But I'm married. I'm no nun. I live in the secular world. What do you expect *me* to do?" My response remains the same. You must be merciful, kind, and virtuous in all you do. These stamp down pride.

Help those in distress, and feel compassion for anyone who sins against you; otherwise, you're just worshiping the idol of greed. Also, never give in to jealousy when God gives someone else some happiness. That's a slap in God's face. Don't do it. Pray instead, and you'll live.

To Eleanor of Aquitaine, Queen of England and Wife of Henry II (1154 or After)

The storm pounding your brain is your panic. It makes you unable to rest. Steady yourself by relying on God. He'll help you now, when you need Him, and so will those around you. Be calm. May God bless and help you in all you do.

To Henry II, King of England and Husband of Eleanor of Aquitaine (1154 or After)

Listen to what the Lord has to say to you. You're a man of many gifts. You'll win heaven for your leading, defending, and providing. But beware the dark bird flying in from the evil north, squawking: "You're powerful. Do whatever you want. Go on—do it. But avoid honesty. It gets you nowhere. It only makes you (who are rightly the Master) a mere slave."

Don't listen to this thief's advice. He's the devil, the one who stole your primal glory after you were first created from dust into beauty when God blew the breath of life into you. Look at your Father instead. Look carefully. He created you. Your good intentions come from Him. You'd be more willing to do good, if not for the influence of the amoral people at your court. Son of God, reject the immorality of these people. Be brave. Call on your Father, because He gladly hands you strength on strength. Live forever, and may you be eternally happy.

***

To Abbot Kuno of St. Disibod (Before 1155)

An immature man always stubbornly refuses to change. He'd rather be a busybody, digging in the private business of others and then broadcasting their secret bad habits. This man must hear the Lord:

> You know how delicious good works are, so why do you turn a deaf ear to their symphony? Examine your own life, and reject the shameless lusts you find in your heart. I bring the lost sheep back to the fold. That's why you should always turn to Me. But you're not doing that. Your rejection of My wounded hands and feet is a slap in My face. You'll have to answer to Me for this.

You'll have to tell Me why your heart's home is not the city I made and cleansed in the blood of the Lamb. And why are you so heavy-handed in disciplining others? Why don't you respect your fellow human beings? You never even worry that you'll break their spirit. Don't you realize that you didn't create them? You protect no one. You bring the oil of blessing to nobody.

That's why your power is declining, but God created you and doesn't want to lose you. You must take these things to heart.

To your question. You asked me, Father, to send you anything I've seen and learned about Disibod, your monastery's patron saint. I've heard some songs about him in one of my visions, and I've included here what I saw and understood:

O mirum admirandum

What a wonderful wonder!
Someone-many-overlooked has triumphed!
His honest heart took him far,
up the mountain, to the living, mystical Voice,
and, Disibod, you'll rise on Doomsday, too,
as you rose on earth,
empowered by the Flower
growing on every bough,
in every land,
all over this globe.

O viriditas digiti Dei

You're the green thumb
God used to plant a garden
that shines on the Hill like a column.
You're wonderful, because you worked hard
in God's endlessly blooming yard!
You're the humble mountain peak
that won't be razed on Doomsday.
You're the pilgrim whose life reminds me
no weapon was strong enough to best you.
You worked wonders, hard at work
in God's eternally green garden!
Glory be to the Father and to the Son and to the Holy Spirit.

O presul vere civitatis

Abbot-bishop of the heavenly city,
at your death, you ascended
to heaven in the sanctuary of the Cornerstone
because you bowed to Him on earth.
Pilgrim! You chose to love Christ,
giving up marriage and embracing
the life of an exile instead.

You're the mountain of the meditative mind.
Your handsome face shone in the mirror of peace.
You hid yourself in the secret garden,
intoxicated by flowers and their fragrance,
shining for God through a latticework of saints.

You're the summit in heaven's gardens,
because, kind confessor, you sold this world
to win an everlasting reward, a life of light.
The living Fountain flowing through your soul
was the purest, brightest river of salvation.
You're a tall tower before God's high altar,
and when you burned incense there,
its smoke perfumed the mountain.

Disibod, through God's Son, your brilliance
created praise in the beautiful music of two choirs.
You stand above us all and feel no shame before the God of life.
With the dew that makes all things green and living,
you shelter and revive those who praise God in this song.
We thank You for Disibod's gentle life and divine endurance,
for his light forever shining in heavenly Jerusalem,
and we praise God for working through Disibod,
and for how much was accomplished through this monk.
Let the citizens of heaven sing in celebration
of those on earth who model their lives after them.

Father, I've answered the questions you've asked me. Now I ask you: Humble yourself before God. Become a poor heartbroken creature in His sight, as I am. Then, when you die on earth, your happiness will last throughout eternity, and you'll be rewarded with the salvation given to those who are honest.

To Emperor Barbarossa (1156)

The One-Who-Is tells you this. My omnipotence destroys the stubbornness of everyone who rebels against Me. I crush their wickedness. Does anyone dare ignore Me? Listen, King, if you want to live. If you don't, My blade will shatter you.

⚜

To the Abbess of Bamberg (After 1157)

Mother, a person who doesn't plow a field to make it grow crops is negligent. She's shirking her work. She's refusing to till the field of her good Master. Didn't God designate the ox and the ass servants of humanity? Yes. Then shouldn't a person do the work God designed? He's got a useful purpose for every person, too. God made no useless human beings.

In the same way that the stars illuminate the sky at night, God made humanity to sparkle. We're created for maturity. We're made to give out light like the sun, the moon, and the stars. If a black cloud covered these, the earth and every creature in it would worry that the end had come.

Daughter of God, the field is yours. Your goodness embraces those in your care. Don't refuse to be their leader. Don't abandon them just because you want a break from the responsibilities of being an abbess, because weeds that choke good growth thrive in idleness. Look at the heavens instead. Remember your purpose, or the devil will deceive you. You might let the black cloud of sin dim your bright reason. If that happens, you might as well be dead.

Here's what you must do. Discipline your daughters. Make them behave. Remember that a child who fears a spanking looks to her mother with respect. Don't be afraid to punish those in your community. If you discipline them, you'll get a bigger reward in the life-to-come, as the Holy Spirit breathes through you.

⚜

To a Nun Named Gertrude (After 1161)

Daughter of God, fix your faith on these words: "The voice of the turtle-dove is heard in our land."[23] This verse refers to the Son of God, who—contrary to natural law—was born from the unplowed earth of the Virgin Mary's flesh. That's when the fragrant, multicolored flowers of the virtues blossomed. This garden of virtues also grew in the prodigal son when he realized that he must run back to his father, who accepted him with the kiss of the Son's humanity.

We hear the turtle-dove's voice when we choose the love of God over the companionship of the world, because only the turtle-dove lives a solitary life after it has lost its mate. You did this, dear daughter, when you abandoned this world's glitter and your riches in it, deciding to put on the truly beautiful shoes of the Gospel of peace and walk the straight-and-narrow way. This is the life of the spirit.

So, celebrate! The Holy Spirit lives in your heart, daughter of Zion. He made you a lily when you rejected the thorns of this world's wealth and chose to live a simple, spirit-centered life. When you entered the order, you glowed like the rose of Jericho.

I rejoice to know you. Everything I hoped for you has been realized. Be happy with me! May your faith rise like a wall decorated with jewels and pearls in God's sight, and may the heavenly choir sing your praises. Rejoice! Be glad in God, because you'll live forever.

⚜

❦

To Count Gerhard of Wertheim (Before 1170)

Although you're God's son and know His loving nature, your mind has strayed, blown by the whirlwind of worry, but don't fret. Things will clear up soon and be bright again.

I'm happy to ask God to remove those problems that make your mother and father suffer so. I'm praying that His grace will protect them now. Remember that God often greatly blesses those who are experiencing tremendous stress. God can also help your brother. He can release him from the chains that bind him. You can even help your brother who has already left this world. Celebrate the Mass thirty times (or get some friends to help you do this).

May God lighten and enlighten your soul, and may you worship Him eternally.

❦

To Abbot Helengerus, who Succeeded Kuno as Abbot of St. Disibod in 1155 (About 1170)

In a spiritual vision from God, this is what I heard. A man consumed by lust can find his soul only if he rejects his unholy impulses, accepts God's way, and follows it. His soul must become his lady and his body his handmaiden. In other words, his soul is like his wife and his body is like his servant.

Remember the Psalmist says, "Happy are those whom you discipline, O LORD, and whom you teach out of your law."[24] Who is meant here? A man with self-control. The Psalmist means that a man must devote himself to his soul with the same passion with which he loves and protects his lady, and that he must, on the other hand, keep his body under control the way he would his servant. Only then will he be truly happy.

If a man fights God like a ferocious bear, but then quits his rage and hungers for the Sun of mercy and integrity, he makes God happy, and God will help him understand His teachings, which will help him discipline God's sheep and show them how to find the fragrant mountain of myrrh.

If you listen to me, you'll learn something. Inside your soul, first you must feel embarrassed when you see yourself for who you are. Sometimes you're an angry, growling, unkind bear, but—since you're weak—you only snarl quietly, under your breath. Sometimes you're a reckless ass. Other times you're like certain birds, which neither soar through the highest heights, nor hug the earth—they neither excel, nor get in trouble. They're just apathetic and mediocre. Finally, in some affairs, you're totally useless—your faithlessness makes you spineless.

Here's what our omnipotent Father has to say about your character:

I don't like your fickleness and your duplicity. I don't like it that your mind snarls at My justice. I don't like the way you refuse to use My wisdom to solve your problems. Instead, you nurse this pettiness inside you. And when you do get some sudden insight, you pray only until you get bored, or tired, and then you quit. You'd rather follow the path that your body wants to take you down. You don't reject your worldly desires. I do sometimes select unstable people (like you) so I can listen to what they're thinking, but if they don't repent, they become useless, and fall.

Don't shun God in your thoughts—you don't know when His sword will find you. I'm only a poor, insignificant woman, but I can see you've ignited a black fire against us at Rupertsberg. Yes, I see this in you, and if you don't put the goodness of your intelligence to work and banish that blackness, forcing it to the outer reaches of nothingness, God's grace and blessing will abandon you while you're in the position of abbot.

Love God's honesty, and you'll know God's love. Trust His miracles, and you'll receive your heavenly reward.

***

From a Letter to Abbot Helengerus of St. Disibod, Delivered by Hildegard as a Sermon There (About 1170)

When God created the world, some bright stars fell with Lucifer into death's darkness, but the planets—who are those fiery angels of truth—stood by God, to serve the inextinguishable fire of the living Light. When the wind quickens this fire, it blazes. That's how the word gets out. All of creation praises God, and His voice is heard; for as the word is to the voice, so the flame of this fire is to the praise of God.

The person who doesn't respect God, can't love, because respect is the flame that spreads divine love like wildfire. And the person who doesn't praise God, can't work, because all of God's creation praises its Creator. God made man and woman in His own image, and He made them to work, like Him, as creators.

Remember? The stars that fell never praised God. They never sang of His beautiful creation. Instead, they spat on God's plan and were reduced to zeroes. God knew the fallen angels couldn't conquer Him. He also knew (before anyone else did) that He would create—through the feminine—something no one else could, not humans and not even angels. Then, after God made man and woman, the fallen angels tempted them and tricked them, and humanity became captive to death.

But the patriarchs of the Old Testament were faithful, and the Unicorn followed after them and satisfied that earliest plan by clothing Himself with flesh in the Virgin's womb. This was something so miraculous that no one but God—not humans, not angels—could make it happen. The Virgin caught the Unicorn, and God made the ivory tower of chastity when He became man. This was God's way of eradicating humanity's death sentence. He overturned the first woman's fall (which began when she let the serpent lead her down the wrong path, throwing the world into the blackest hole) and led humanity out by shining sunlight on the Virgin, leaving the miserable devil confounded in hell.

God created everything for a reason. When we choose good, God helps us serve Him well, but if we choose evil, we risk an ambush by the devil in the north. Don't forget that we have two wings of wisdom, the knowledge of good and evil. They work together in a mysterious symbiosis, the way a word can't live apart from a voice, and a voice can't speak without words. Sometimes you hear someone's voice but can't make out their words, but when words and voice work together, we can understand all things (both helpful and useless). Always try to learn new things, then, because that's as necessary to wisdom as internal organs are to being healthy.

Here's how we learn to work. First we suck our mother's breast-milk, then we're content to mouth ground-up food, we begin to chew with our teeth next, and then we start selecting what we eat, refusing what we don't like. This is how the baby becomes a man, filled with knowledge. He forgets he drank his mother's milk or ate mushy baby-food and grows up to know truth.

The progression of knowledge can be compared to these biblical stages. The age of milk came first, before the flood. Noah lived during the age of pabulum, and Abraham came next; this signifies the time when the child chews with molars and begins choosing her own food. The age of Moses marks the end of childish days, because he foreshadowed the coming of Christ. Finally, the new, mature age began with the coming of God's Son, through the cleansing, life-giving water of redemption.

Christ attracted two planets to Himself—virgins and monks—and they rose with Him, and miracles abounded. Just as the Son of God hid in the Virgin's womb to take on foreign flesh, He welcomes to Himself a second foreign nature in the nuns and monks who, like Him, reject this vain world.

Remember that Wisdom never rushes. Even God's Son was gradually revealed to creation, in diverse ways. Wisdom's never in a hurry. It always looks ahead to make sure nothing's wrong with its plans. A foolish person does just the opposite. Whatever pops into their head, they do right then, and their work often fails, like the impetuous angel's. He overestimated his own importance and crashed right then into the darkest lake, saying goodbye forever to anything that was worth something, as he sank into the endlessly smoking black fire.

But the planets (the nuns and monks) keep on revolving, doing honorable, reverent things, as required by their religious orders. Then a dictator came to power, who loved to listen to the old Serpent. That's when we entered this womanish time, which is almost as bad as the first fall. Justice is now as puny as the weakness of woman.

Hear this warning. Consider the early history of your monastery, its current health, and its probable future. Born in the fiery sun, this community was strong and spiritual, dead to the world and its temptations. Its members embraced simplicity. Like eagles, they looked at heaven, and in that brightness, they burned brilliantly for God and for all humanity. They went from virtue to virtue and were much praised. They lived out the fragrance of St. Benedict's *Rule*, rejecting this world's empty pleasures. In Christ's humility, they lived singular lives.

But then the fog of pride clouded their bright good works, like a cloud dimming the sun and blocking it out. Storms came and disordered them, but later they got back on their feet, only to have the smog of pride return again to obscure the fire of spiritual discipline and good behavior taught by St. Benedict's *Rule*. To this day, these incompatibilities persist here, warping this community with the unholy mix of the spiritual and the secular.

This sermon is for those who think the glittery show of this world and the monastic life are one and the same thing. Never. Wish it all you want, but it won't make it true. If you believe this, you're like the Samaritans, bowing to strange gods. The high principles of St. Benedict's *Rule* are a fiery sun, and those who try mixing these with the world's concerns are clouds.

Listen. Remember that obedience to St. Benedict's *Rule* is your spiritual weapon. Your enemies are stubbornness, insubordination, pride, and permissiveness. You must follow the *Rule*'s wise, biblical guidelines. Model yourself after the worthy knight who fell to his knees, surrounded by his enemies, but kept on fighting in that position until he could stand again to do battle. You must keep on fighting! Then, like the knight, you'll find your strength renewed.

Although the age of utter angst and devastation has not yet come (when the winepress will completely squeeze the juice from the grapes), we do already live in a sordid time. Look to God, and He'll help you. A time of renewed morality is coming, when people will fix their eyes on that first Sunrise. The monastic community will long for God, and they'll persist in kindness. Then the people will shout, "The voice of the turtle-dove is heard in our land."[25] That voice belongs to those who follow God. They walk the straight path, glancing behind them at the past to see what was helpful and what was useless. This contemplation gives God's doves the wisdom to escape the hungry hawk, for they know to fly far away when they see the hawk's reflection in the water.

Listen to one last point. You've still got some brightness in you, but it's only a flickering sort of light. You've got good intentions, and you fear God; but your immaturity makes your candle sputter. You're unsteady. Beware of the stinking black corruption that hates God and humanity. The devil loves nothing more than this, when he can throw his spear through you, caught in sin.

So, although I'm only a weak, worthless woman, I saw and heard these words in a mystic vision. Ever since I was a child, God has used these visions to teach me. I was told to get out of my sickbed and preach these things in person here at your monastery. That's why you must not look down on them or reject them. If you do, you'll die on earth.

May the Holy Spirit build His sanctuary in you. May you come to a good end. Your monastery has been blessed, because God has brought you together, to serve Him. Don't do anything that will make you feel ashamed, or God will punish you. He has protected you in times of danger, but if you focus on your own will and on getting your way—if you refuse to look to God, bad things will happen to you.

Letter to the Belgian Monk Guibert (1175)

The words I speak are never my own, and they don't belong to any other human being, either. I report what I see in celestial visions. As a servant of God, you understand what it's like to see God reflected in faith's mirror. Placed in a frame, as the soul is put in a fragile body, a mirror shows what's in front of it, the way the soul sees through faith. On this earthly pilgrimage, the soul, then, guides the body, by meditating on heavenly matters.

Listen, son of God, to what the undying Light says. Humans are heavenly and earthly. We're heavenly because our bright souls think rationally, and we're weak and earth-bound because we also know dark lusts. The more a person notices and accepts the good in themselves, the more they love God. It's like when a person sees their dirty face in a mirror—they wash it because they want to make it clean. This is the person who chases life's empty pleasures. They should let good knowledge wake them up and cleanse their soul. When they feel godly sorrow, they must repent. But if you know you're dirty, and still don't resist sin, you're letting the blackbirds of evil totally pollute your soul.

I—an insignificant woman—write these words to you, God's faithful servant, from a genuine vision. Even if God raised my body up as He does my spirit in my visions, I'd still be afraid, because, though cloistered from a very young age, I'm only human.

Some people who see visions blow their own horns with them, and pride ruins their lives. Others see visions but understand that their wisdom comes from God. I'm one of these. I'm human, and I know it. St. Paul felt the same way. He was an exceptionally talented, articulate preacher—much better at preaching than the others, in fact—but he never put on airs. Instead, he and the apostle John were humble. Through their humility, they connected intimately with God's divinity, and saw much.

I've always known I'm merely a fragile creature who speaks what God reveals. Otherwise, how could He use me? His ways bring glory to His name, not to ours. Still, I'm a hesitant person, afraid and insecure in ways others may not see. But I lift my soul to God, because I know He raises me up each time like a feather, which on its own weighs nothing, and I fly on the breath of God. However, I never completely understand what I see in my visions, because the Fall left every person's soul and body incomplete.

I'm now over seventy years old, but ever since I was a child, I've seen what God has shown me. He doesn't reveal things to me through any of my five senses. I don't hear these visions with my physical ears, nor do I understand them with my mind. God shows these mysteries directly to my soul, when I'm wide awake, night and day. I never see them in nor suffer from the infirmity of ecstasy. Instead, God raises me up to the heavens, into the highest winds, and my sight roves over the world, among many peoples, as clouds shift below me and creation moves. In spite of these visions, my body is always in pain, and I'm often near death; but God sustains me.

My spirit is ever illuminated by what I call the shadow of the living Light. It has no physical limitations whatsoever and is much brighter than a cloud through which the sun shines. I can never predict when or how I'll see it. As water reflects the sun, the moon, and the stars, this shadow of the living Light reflects God's Word, sermons, virtues, and the things that humans do.

Whatever I see in that Light's shadow stays in my mind for a long time, stored away. I see and understand, hear and know at the same time. I only know what I see in these visions, because I'm untaught. I record what I see and hear, without adding my own words, and my Latin is unrefined, because that's how I hear it in my visions. I've not been taught to write like a philosopher. Also, my visions are filled with images and sounds that are nothing like words spoken by any human. They're more like a blazing fire and a cloud floating through a clear sky. I can't comprehend this Light's shadow any better than I can look right at the sun.

Also, sometimes in that shadow (but not very often) I see another light. This is the living Light I spoke of earlier. I'm even less able to explain what this Light is like in comparison to the other. But I can say that when I look at it, every feeling of sadness disappears, and my every ache leaves me. I'm no longer an old, sick woman. I become young again.

I'm always sick, and sometimes that means I don't feel well enough at first to write down what I see. But, then, I get a taste of the vision and am so altered, as I said, that I lose all my grief and pain in that great nothingness. My spirit gulps these down from the bottomless cup of the Fountain.

I should mention that that first light I described to you (the *shadow* of the living Light) is something I always see. It's like looking at a sparkling sky, seen through a shining cloud. In this shadow of light, I see the things I always speak about. Its lucidity tells me what to say to those who ask me questions. A vision also showed me that I should title my first book *Scivias*, because it was created—not from the teaching of any person—but by the living Light.

I had a vision about crowns, too. In it, I saw that virginity needed a symbol, because—while the different orders of the church have distinct symbols—virginity only had the black veil and the sign of the cross. I saw that virgins should cover their heads with a white veil, symbolizing humanity's innocence in Eden and the virgins' chastity, and that they should wear a simple tri-color crown, representing the Trinity. On the front of this crown should be the Lamb of God; on the right, one of the cherubim; on the left, an angel; and on the back, a man.

I turn to God, because He's alive and omnipresent, and I'm nothing. I know nothing, and I am nothing—and I give these misgivings over to Him, and He protects me from all evil. I hope you'll pray for me, too. I hope everyone there with you will join you in praying for me, too. Pray that I'll continue to grow in God and serve Him in a genuine, happy way.

Finally, think about the eagle. You want to follow God and know Him well, so you'll understand this story. The eagle soars through the sky on two mighty wings. Since both of these are imperative for flying, if one of his wings is injured, the eagle plunges to the earth and stays there. Like the eagle, we've got the two strong wings of wisdom, the one on the right—the knowledge of good, and the one on the left—the knowledge of evil. These provide us with checks and balances that keep our souls from straying.

Dear son of God, may the Lord lift the wings of your knowledge. Never give in to sin. Stick to the right path. The heavenly choir will sing your praises then. May you and all those with you there be blessed.

To Count Philip of Flanders (1175)

Son of God—and you are His son because He made you when He made the first man—hear the words I saw and heard in my alert soul when I turned to the living Light with your questions about your upcoming crusade to Jerusalem. When Adam disobeyed God by listening to the Serpent, God evicted him from Eden. Our God is a God of integrity. Then God sent the flood to obliterate those who had forgotten Him. And rightly so. But even then He saved everyone who loved Him. And the gentle Lamb, God's Son, bled on the cross to cleanse us from our sins, when we repent.

So, son of God, look to God as the eagle looks at the sun—with the eye of integrity—and you'll make good decisions, uncorrupted by selfishness. If you don't do this, the Commander of all may ask you, "Why did you go crusading and kill your neighbor without consulting Me?" You're also responsible for controlling those whose anger makes them itch to commit homicide, and you must yourself contemplate the things you've ignored, such as your sins and unfair decisions. Make the sign of the cross and come back to God, the way and the truth. He never wants a sinner to die. He wants every person to turn from the wrong way and live.

A final word. If the godless try to annihilate the fountain of faith, you must stand firm, as best you can, in God's grace. The worries of your soul look like a sunrise to me. They're a good thing. They show you have a penitent heart. May the Holy Spirit bless it and make you blaze like the sun. Seek God. Serve Him and Him alone, and you'll live in the highest happiness eternally.

To the Prelates at Mainz (1178 or 1179)

God—who is the ultimate Artist—created a vision in my soul before I was born, and this vision urges me to write this letter in answer to the interdict placed on us by those in authority. A certain nobleman was buried by his priest in our monastery without controversy, but afterwards, we were commanded to dig him up and take him away from hallowed ground.

This news terrified me, so I looked as I always do to the living Light and saw that I should not comply with this order, because the dead man had in fact confessed his sins and died having obtained absolution. We do not resist out of disrespect; instead, we don't want it to look as if a womanly belligerence leads us to contradict Christ's sacraments. To show our obedience insofar as we are able to comply, we have stopped singing, as ordered.

But my sisters and I find this prohibition more than a little depressing. That's why I'm writing you now, because my vision told me: *It's not right for you to bow to human words forcing you to give up singing and praising God. You must go back to the prelates at Mainz and ask them to remove their injunction.* I also heard in my vision that I'd made a mistake in not humbling myself and asking my superiors to allow us to take part in communion. And I saw that, since the injunction, we've been celebrating the *Opus Dei* wrongly, by reading it instead of singing it. That's why I'm writing you now, to let you know what God showed me in my vision.

A voice emanating from the living Light made me think on David's psalm, which says: "Praise him with trumpet sound; praise him with lute and harp! Let everything that breathes praise the LORD! Praise the LORD!"[26] These visible words teach us invisible spiritual lessons. When we sing, we repossess some of the Eden that we lost when Adam fell.

That's why the Holy Spirit inspired prophets to write songs, to touch the hearts of all who hear them. The prophets were also called to make different kinds of musical instruments to accompany these songs of praise, enriching them. When we hear the splendid music that these instruments make, absorbing the meaning of the psalms' words, we learn more about spiritual truths alive within us.

Music stirs our hearts and engages our souls in ways we can't describe. When this happens, we are taken beyond our earthly banishment back to the divine melody Adam knew when he sang with the angels, when he was whole in God, before his exile. In fact, before Adam refused God's fragrant flower of obedience, his voice was the best on earth, because he was made by God's green thumb, who is the Holy Spirit. And if Adam had never lost the harmony God first gave him, the mortal fragilities that we all possess today could never have survived hearing the booming resonance of that original voice.

Of course it infuriates the devil that his clever schemes went wrong, and he forever plots how to make humanity stop singing. Even in church. The devil wants to thwart confession, stop forgiveness, and silence our songs of praise, because they frighten him. In their place he wants to put gossip, arguments, and the suppression of true freedom.

Therefore, you must meet to discuss the injunction you have put on us, which is not only a heavy burden for my community but also shushes the praise of God and stops the giving-and-receiving of divine sacraments. You must decide whether or not you are commanding this out of a pure love for God or from resentment, bitterness, and a desire to get even. Make sure it's not Satan driving your decision.

Remember that singing is our best hope to hear divine harmony again.

Then I heard a voice ask, "Who made heaven?" God. "Who lets the faithful into heaven?" God. "Is anyone like God?" No. That's why, men of faith, you mustn't oppose God, because He'll crush you in His scrutiny. But this is a weak, womanly age, and the Church is neither as truthful nor as kind as it should be. However, God is at work. Like a female warrior, God fights to vanquish every type of unfairness on earth.

–5–

Physica and Causes and Cures

Love cherishes all things,
designs all things,
supports all things,
keeps all things—
high and low—
and seals her King's devotion
with the peace of a kiss.
—Hildegard, *Symphonia*

INTRODUCTION TO *PHYSICA* AND *CAUSES AND CURES*

ILDEGARD'S COSMOLOGY and physiology are based on the four-humor, four-element approach dating back to the ancient Greeks. She believed a person's health depended on the balance of the four basic fluids, the "humors" of blood, yellow bile, phlegm, and black bile. We give this ancient concept a nod today when we say that someone is "good-humored."

Because Hildegard saw the human body as a microcosm of the universe, she saw that these four humors were echoed in the four elements of air, fire, water, and earth: She understood blood as the humor associated with air and hot-and-moist elements, resulting in a "sanguine" (happy, loving, generous) temperament; yellow bile was associated with fire and hot-and-dry elements, resulting in a "choleric" (unforgiving, bitter, violent) temperament; phlegm was associated with water and cold-and-moist elements, resulting in a "phlegmatic" (sluggish, unemotional, withdrawn) temperament; and black bile was associated with earth and cold-and-dry elements, resulting in a "melancholic" (depressive) temperament.

As she does with so much of the tradition she inherited, Hildegard presents this classic schema with an original twist. Usually, the two "warm" elements, air and fire, were thought masculine, and the two "cold" elements, water and earth, were held to be feminine. But Hildegard believed that she had an intense affinity with air. This may have been a twelfth-century effort by the physician Hildegard to—if not heal—at least diagnose herself. She believed that her "airy" (more active and more cerebral) female temperament and physique made her spiritually more open to visions and physically more susceptible to illness. Perhaps the most famous metaphor for her airy self-perception is when she describes herself as "a feather on the breath of God."

Hildegard also made much use of the medieval *Bestiary*, often called *The Book of the Beasts*. To the modern mind with its scientific underpinnings, the medieval *Bestiary* is a strange mish-mash of fantastic animal lore, but to anyone in the Middle Ages, this collection of natural history was taken very seriously as a textbook of Christian mores. In addition to redacting her own bestiary in her

Physica, Hildegard also filled her writings with allusions to this work. It pays to look at the curious medieval text behind some of these references.

When Hildegard refers to the eagle's sharp sight, her audience knew the full story by oral tradition. This entertaining legend, first found in the *Physiologus* (or *Naturalist*, c. AD 100), recounts that when an eagle notices that its once-keen eyes are opaque with age and its wings heavy, the old bird flies up to the sun to burn away this dimness. Its wings burst Phoenix-like into flame, and then it falls, submerging itself three times in a fountain to become a new creature. The obvious moral drawn from this story is that in the fountain of the Lord comes spiritual healing. The Gospelist John was often compared with the eagle, too, because, just as the eagle with its powerful eyes could look on the sun (the Son) and not only live but also become rejuvenated, John was able to look on (and perceive) the Savior's divinity with a uniquely strong, renewing poetic vision.[27] Allusions to the eagle in this Hildegard reader are found in the "Song for Mary" (from vision thirteen of *Scivias*), in the first letter to the abbot of Busendorf, in the letter (also sermon) to Abbot Helengerus, in the letter to Guibert, and in the letter to Count Philip.

The letter-sermon to Abbot Helengerus also contains references to the unicorn and to the turtle-dove. The unicorn in the *Bestiary* is associated with Christ and is known for its bravery. This animal's single horn is said to show that Christ and His Father are one, and this mythical beast is also linked with virginity, a primary focus for Hildegard, because the only way to capture a unicorn (as every medieval person knew) is to lure it with a virgin. The otherwise-uncatchable unicorn will lay its head in her lap and rest there.

The turtle-dove, on the other hand, stands for chastity-in-widowhood and a virgin's steadfast loyalty to Christ. The *Bestiary* tells the story of the turtle-dove, who—when its mate dies—refuses anyone else, eschewing sex forever after the loss of its partner, to whom she remains loyal, even in death. Hildegard alludes to the story of the turtle-dove in her letter to the nun Gertrude in this reader. Her obvious relish in using this particular story from the *Bestiary* shows that, as in her songs and theological prose works, one of Hildegard's leitmotifs is always the exalted and Christlike spiritual and physical life of the virgin.

On the Four Elements

God made the four elements, earth, air, water, and fire, and they're the cosmic building-blocks of this world. Each person is also made up of these. The elements are interdependent, impossible to break down into separate components, and they profoundly impact, not only the world, but also each human. Their dispersal throughout the cosmos changes our world, and their interaction within every person determines that person's temperament.

Fire gives us warmth, air provides our breath, water makes our blood, and earth gives us our tissue, muscles, and bones. Fire also gives us our sight, air our hearing, water our ability to move, and earth our groundedness in walking. When these four elements are ordered correctly, heat and moisture come and go throughout the earth at just the right times and in just the right amounts, helping crops grow and nourishing the world and everything in it.

However, if the four elements come too much all at once, out of order and out of season, they rip the world apart and make it sick. Likewise, the elements must be balanced within each person, or that person becomes sick and can die. For example, Adam's fall transformed the warm-moist personality we were originally given into a phlegmatic, lazy, sinning temperament.

Causes and Cures

On Humanity's Interdependency with Nature

Why did God create the world out of earth, air, water, and fire? To bring glory to His divine name. He used the wind to wake up the world. Then He used stars to light the earth, and He filled it with different creatures. God made sure to give us everything we need to thrive, and He also gave us much power, because nature nourishes us in so many ways. The relationship between us and creation must be symbiotic, because humanity can't live without the nature that God made.

Physica

On Overeating

Don't stress your body with overeating. Your stomach gets irritated when you eat too much or indulge in unhealthy foods. Also, your bladder can get inflamed if you drink unhealthy drinks. These will send acidic juices to the intestines and a bad smoke to your spleen, which will then swell and get sore. The swelling and discomfort of your spleen will make your heart hurt, and a mucus will form around it. The heart will try to heal itself, but if your poor nutrition continues, the acidic juices in your intestines and spleen will increase, weakening your heart. At some point, they'll mix with black bile. This unhealthy concoction of juices will then head towards your heart with rage, and a dark smoke will settle there.

Heart problems result. Sometimes people who've had this happen to them become depressed and grumpy. They may lose their appetite all at once, drop weight, and feel zapped of energy.

Causes and Cures

On Depression

People panic when they feel their body is in danger—everything pulls in on itself and gets smaller. Everything contracts—the heart, the liver, and the blood vessels. This constriction releases a fog that hovers over the heart and darkens it. The person's blood sours.

This is how a person becomes sad. The depressed person finds that tears rise like smoke and sting their eyes. These tears dehydrate the blood, reducing a person's flesh. Such tears of sadness can make a person sick, just as rotten food can. They dim the eyes.

Tears of joy, however, are gentler on the body. The sad soul mustn't forget who made the world and who made humans pilgrims on it. We must cry from the joy of knowing that God loves us. Tears of joy are never injurious.

Causes and Cures

On Spelt

A warm breakfast is important. The first thing a person eats in the morning should include something made from flour, because dry foods make a body strong, as do fruits. A healthy person can, however, wait to eat breakfast at noon, because this will improve their digestion. But if a person is sick or weak, they must eat breakfast first thing, to give them strength.

Wheat is hot and rich. It's a complete food. Flour must be made from wheat without sifting out the bran, or the result will be a loaf of anemic bread. Of all the grains that can be made into flour or porridge, spelt is the best, because it's hot, healthy, and nourishing. It warms the blood, sticks to the backbone, and is easy on the digestive tract, too. It will strengthen you and make you happy.

It doesn't matter how you prepare spelt. It's good for you regardless. Also, if someone is sick, you can boil spelt and mix it with egg and lard to make a tasty, potent medicine.

Causes and Cures and *Physica*

On Migraines

An excess of black bile or sometimes the imbalance of the other humors causes migraines. These pains affect one side of the head or the other. When the migraine is caused by black bile, the left side of the head hurts. If the migraine is caused by a dominance of the bad qualities of the other three humors, the right side of the head aches. If migraines radiated their agony throughout the entire head, no person could bear it. This is a very hard illness to treat.

Causes and Cures

On Garlic

Garlic is hot in nature, and vibrant, because it grows down low, in the dew. It's healthier to eat than leeks, and everyone—both sick and well—should eat raw garlic. Cooking ruins the flavor. But eating too much garlic is also unhealthy. It makes a person's blood excessively hot. Also, old garlic is no good because it's lost its vitality.

Physica

On the Ocean

The ocean makes rivers, which in turn water the earth the same way a person's body is irrigated by the blood rushing through their veins.

Physica

On the Apple Tree

The apple tree has a hot, moist nature, and is a very good medicine. If someone has a migraine, a sick liver or spleen, or indigestion, they should gather the tender shoots of the apple tree and put them in a jar of olive oil. Then place this mixture out in the sun, to heat up. Drinking this regularly before bed will lessen headaches and other pains.

Apples themselves are easy to digest and grow with the dew. They're fine to eat raw, unless a person is sick. When cooked or dried, apples are good for anyone.

Physica

–6–

The Book of Life's Merits

Eleven hundred years after God was incarnated as Christ,
the solid teaching of the apostles, plus the fiery integrity
and spirituality of the early Christians had faded
into nothing but a waffling.
—Hildegard, from an autobiographical section of her *Vita*

INTRODUCTION TO *THE BOOK OF LIFE'S MERITS*

THIS BOOK'S SIX VISIONS focus on the temptations every Christian encounters and how God can help those who love Him resist these. Hildegard details thirty-five vices, plus their punishments and fitting acts of penance. Traditionally, the vices were presented as all-female (partly because the Latin nouns for these abstract concepts are feminine), but Hildegard presents the sins mostly as hideous creatures that are a mix of human and beast. In doing so, she made sin as ugly as possible and also avoided denigrating women.

In *The Book of Life's Merits*, joy is praised as the earthly reward for obeying God. Hildegard also shows that the spiritual rebels who choose not to follow God experience a worldly sadness that can neither see nor participate in the ubiquitous divine happiness. The disobedient are seen as literally dry and lifeless. Perhaps this book's focus on human stubbornness and frailties resulted from Hildegard's writing it in the years after her bitter early-1150s arguments with the Disibodenberg monks (and with a few nuns) over her decision to leave Disibod and found the Rupertsberg convent.

The Cosmic Man and His Trumpet

When I was sixty, I saw another powerful vision. It was wondrous, and I worked five years to write it down. In the 1158th year after the Lord was incarnated on earth, during the reign of Emperor Barbarossa, I heard a voice speaking to me from heaven. It said,

> Visions have been your teacher since your earliest days. Some of your visions were like milk, others like semi-liquid baby food, and still others like solid food. Articulate now what you hear Me say. Don't rely on yourself. Write down what you see and hear.

So I did.

I saw a very tall man. His head and shoulders were above the highest clouds. His torso was in a white cloud below this, while his upper legs were in the earth's atmosphere. From the knees down, he was planted in the earth, and his feet were rooted in the deepest waters of the abyss, which represent the virtues and their power. They are the antidotes to sin, because they have the might to make anything whole. They do this by cleansing whatever they touch and making it holy. They nurture and sustain the world, and they bear all things. Everything on earth steeps in the moisture of the virtues and is made strong, in the same way that the soul makes the body moist and healthy, regenerating it.

The tall man stood and looked East and South, but when I tried to see who he was, his face was too bright, so I couldn't see him clearly. Next to his mouth was a white cloud that looked like a trumpet, and many sounds floated out of it. When the tall man blew this trumpet, three winds flew out of it, and each wind had a cloud with it—one fiery, one stormy, and one bright.

The stormy-cloud wind and the sunny-cloud wind dropped down to the man's chest and settled there, while the fiery-cloud wind stayed near his face. In this fiery cloud was a community and it glowed, because they were watching the tablet on which the Lord wrote His commandments. This tablet had wings on every side, and flew, and the crowd watched it carefully. Their gazing on God's wise Scripture gave them the strength to make wonderful music. During all this, the cosmic man was inspecting the globe from top to bottom.

The Black Cloud and Vomiting Devil

I also saw a black cloud blow in from the North. It was dry and joyless, because it lacked all sun. The dark cloud held evil spirits that kept drifting here and there, trying to tempt people into sin, but when they saw the tall man, they felt ashamed.

I heard the old serpent shout, "I'll fight my enemies with everything in my power!" and then he vomited chunks of infected throw up all over all the people. Next, he made fun of them, saying, "You think you're so good, so full of light and good works. I'll make you disgusting," and he heaved again, sending more revolting black vomit splattering on the earth.

In this puke, I saw seven sins. The first was love-of-the-world, the second was shallowness, the third was showiness, the fourth was hardheartedness, the fifth was laziness, the sixth was anger, and the seventh was lusting-after-pleasure.

The Conversation Between Love-of-the-World and Agape Love

Love-of-the-world was as naked as a savage would be. Its arms and legs wrapped around the trunk of a tree blooming wildly. Its skin was dark, and it greedily plucked the tree's blossoms until its arms and hands were stuffed with flowers. Then it boasted,

> I'm successful! I rule the world! I'm never going to be a with-ered-up has-been—no, I won't—because look at all this lovely greenness in my hands. See? I'll never be old. I'll always be young. I'm going to enjoy the beauty of this world as long as I can. I've got no interest in your descriptions of a heaven I've never seen. They mean nothing to me!

As soon as Love-of-the-world had said this, the tree dried up, crashing to the ground, falling into the darkness, and taking the figure with it.

Agape Love spoke from the stormy cloud that represents the man-made problems of this world:

> Love-of-the-world, you're stupid. Why crave a life as short as an ember among ashes? Why wish to live-and-age on earth and not look for eternal life? It doesn't matter how many flowers you pick, you're still going to fall into the flaming lake of hell. You're like a worm, living sans light, here one day and gone the next, if the mud dries up. You're destined for darkness, for you live only for the moment—which soon enough turns to hay. You think I reject life? I don't. I'm the giver of every joy. I'm every harmony. But I condemn you. The virtues are reflected in me, and the faithful see themselves there.

The Conversation Between Shallowness and Self-Control

The second image looked something like a hunting-dog standing on its hind legs, tail wagging. It asked, "What? Why be only a little happy? Are you telling me I don't deserve the best life I can get? Why focus on death? Forget that—nobody lives forever. Why not be happy while we can?"

Self-control said to this beastlike creature:

Shallowness, you're a crook! At the first strong wind, you'll be blown away. You're as friendly as a dog and people are attracted to you, but you give them nothing but bad advice, because you encourage them to do whatever they feel like doing. This wounds others. Because you follow the law, you're able to trap people more readily. But you know nothing of right and wrong. You forget ethics. On the other hand, I'm the sash of holiness and the robe of integrity and am often the king's wedding guest.

The Conversation Between Showiness and Modesty

The third figure was not unlike a man with black hair, but it had a beak for a nose, bear-paws for hands, and griffin-claws for feet. Its outfit was dingy. This thing squawked:

Come on, smile! Don't be so serious. Wouldn't you rather play than be morose? It's much more fun, and who said having fun's a sin? Aren't those who know God supposed to rejoice and be glad? Isn't heaven and all of God's creation on earth full of divine joy? So am I! If I were sad all the time, who'd want to be my friend? Forget that! All I want to do is have some fun. I'm going to try it all, and be joyful. God made the very air that brings beautiful sounds to my ears, and He gave the flowers their green vibrancy that my eyes enjoy. Why shouldn't I celebrate?

Modesty said to this grotesque figure:

Showiness, you're like the sound of two hands clapping. You make joke after joke, as easily as another person breathes. But you're not really funny. You're idolatry, because you're only interested in getting your own way. The hook of your nose shows that you want to attract people to you. You're starved to be noticed. You act like someone who's always dying—for attention. You're so vain! I burn with shame when I think how you act. You're too loud, while I conceal myself under one of the cherubim. Your bear-hands and griffin-feet mean you make others follow your dirty ways. Your will is both human and beastlike, but I read to learn God's secrets, as they are written down in holy books. My eyes are innocent. I'm honest, and this helps me see God's will, while you run from it, blind.

The Conversation Between Hardheartedness and Mercy

The fourth figure was like dark smoke shaped like a large person, but with no limbs. It never moved. It had huge black eyes and spent all its time complaining:

What have I ever dreamed up? What have I created? Zilch. So why work? Why should I knock myself out? I just won't do it! I never pay attention to others unless helping them helps me. Let God the Creator provide our every need. I'm only interested in what's in it for me. I refuse to do anything else, good or evil. Why be compassionate? What good would it do *me*? I'm looking out for number one! Let everyone else look out for themselves, too.

Mercy said to the fourth:

Hardheartedness, what did you say? You don't deserve to be human. Your lack of compassion makes you a stone, as bitter as the blackest smoke. The only thing you possess is a pair of cruel black eyes, while I, Mercy, am the sweetest-smelling green plant. I'm not all dried up like you. You exclude others from your life, but I've got a good heart and want to help others. If someone is broken, I'm there. If someone hurts, I listen. Why? Because I take that first *Let there be* literally.

The Conversation Between Laziness and Victory

The fifth figure had the spineless body of a worm, and its head was humanlike, except that its left ear was as huge as a head, and hare-shaped. This creature squirmed like a baby in its hole. When it spoke, its voice quavered:

I'm going to be nice to everyone. I won't rush to do anything, because then I might offend someone, and then I might be rejected by my friends, and then I might be alone. I'm going to sit right here and praise my rich, upper-class friends, yes, I will. Why converse with holy people? What good would that do me? I want to make nice with everyone so I can avoid any type of suffering, yes—I'd rather lie than speak the truth and get hurt. Those who fight for truth are sometimes killed, too. That's not for me!

Victory said to the fifth,

Laziness, you stepped off the right path with your first lie. You're just not truthful. I'll hit you with my sword and make sure you have very little success. You can grab all the world's empti-

ness you want, but I prefer visiting the sparkling Fountain. I fight
the devil with Scriptural mysteries.

The Conversation Between Anger and Patience

The sixth figure had the face of a man and the mouth of a scorpion.
Its eyes were perverse, because its pupils were the tiniest of dots inside
very large whites. It had human arms, clawlike hands, and long,
curving fingernails, and was bald and naked. It had a torso like a crab,
shins like locusts, and feet like snakes. It had somehow gotten snarled
in a mill-wheel that kept on spinning and spinning. As this sixth
creature turned, it spat out words of fire:

> I'll run over anyone or anything bothering me. You hear me? You
> won't injure me!—I won't let it happen—no, I won't—why should
> I? Huh? Do anything you want, but you'd better not aggravate me.
> I'm telling you. If you do—are you listening?—I'll grab my sharpest
> sword and stab you. Make me mad, and I'll take my heaviest stick
> and beat you with it. I'm telling you—don't mess with me.

Patience said to the sixth,

> Anger, you live in darkness and deception. You even deceive
> yourself. Your hands are twisted with rage. Your long fingernails
> curve from your greediness that reaches out to attack others' hard
> work. You're naked because you don't have on the shirt of correc-
> tion, and also because sometimes your abusive words are
> deafening, and obvious to all. But I'm a gentle breeze bringing a
> pleasant rain, flowers, and the virtues' fruits. I always finish what
> I start, and I don't stomp on anybody. But if you build a tower
> with your pride, count on this. It will be destroyed by one small,
> quiet word from me. I'm eternal.

The Conversation Between Lusting-after-Pleasure and Desire-for-God

The top half of the seventh figure looked like a naked man, but its hands were an ape's. From the waist down, it was goat-shaped. I couldn't see its feet because they were buried in darkness. It laughed:

I live the good life. God made everything, so why should I go without? He's the One who gave me these wonderful days, so why shouldn't I make the most of them? You're going to tell me not to revel in the pleasures of my flesh? I'm one of those who knows how much life has to offer. Others are too blind to see life's joys, but I'm certainly not one of those. I'm going to live every day to the fullest!

Desire-for-God said to the seventh,

Lusting-after-pleasure, don't you see you're naked? Why aren't you red in the face? Your lifestyle is blind, indecisive, and plain dumb. Your actions violate every moral truth, as well as the common sense surrounding self-esteem and kindness to others. Go ahead, be dry as straw. You've got a good brain, but you've chosen to walk the most illogical path, your feet in darkness. Stop being a beast. You're reacting to deeply held anger. Stop lying to yourself. It makes you unstable. Look at me. I'm friends with angels. I need the eternal, unchanging happiness of divine harmony. Don't you?

The tall man stretching from oceans to heavens then said to all with ears:

Hear what I have to say. Listen and obey. Practice repentance. Asking for forgiveness must become your way of life,

HILDEGARD of BINGEN

because God revealed Himself to you in His Son. You must make confession a genuine habit. If you don't, I'll take my rod and punish you.

On Anger

Anger is the worst fault. It's the devil's heart. An angry person gnaws away every virtuous grain, devouring everything that's germinating.

Anger is a stubborn thief. It gnashes its teeth at people because of their worthy gifts from God. It steals whatever it can snatch.

Anger starts controversy whenever it can. Anger is a dragon burning up whatever it can, wherever it goes. In anger, wisdom is unwise, patience strains with impatience, and temperance rushes around without moderation.

Anger is bitterness. It rejects the goodness and sweetness in God's teachings and vomits it all up. It's the murderer dividing body and soul and not allowing them to be together. It's also a hard, immovable rock, because it grinds away every decent, honest thing. When anger overcomes someone, it overcomes them with great madness, thinking neither about earthly things nor about heavenly things while it shatters the life of another person who was made in God's image.

Anger attracts great pain to itself.

Avoid this sin if you want your soul to live in God. Avoid it, so you don't wound your soul seriously. Repent while you can.

On Depression

I saw Ungodly Sadness. I saw a woman with her back against a tree, its leaves completely shriveled up. The tree's branches twisted around her forehead, neck, and throat and wrapped around her arms and pinned them both close to her body. Her hands hung limp among the mass of vines, and she was naked except for the tangled brown thicket around her body. None of it was green.

Demons came in a sour black cloud and swarmed over her. She threw her head back and moaned:

> I regret the day I was born. I hate my life! Can anyone help me? Can anyone set me free? If God could, then why did He let me be hurt to begin with? My trust in Him is useless. If God is my God, then why won't He rescue me? Where is grace? Why does God refuse me everything good?
>
> I don't know who I am anymore. I was conceived and born in sadness, and my days are now hopeless and joyless. What good is a life of pain? Why was I ever born? Nothing good ever happens to me!

Then Divine Joy said to Ungodly Sadness:

> Look at the sun and the moon and the stars, and every green thing on earth. Look at them and remember how lucky you are. You have these. God gave them to you, even though humans have decided to sin against Him everywhere, openly. You've chosen to call day night, salvation damnation, and every blessing not-good-enough. The world's not bad. Your attitude is.
>
> Those who choose to be ungrateful attract the kind of sorrow that does their souls no good, but those who praise God's abundant gifts always gather and enjoy the world's roses and lilies and everything green.

On Turning to God

"I love you, O LORD, my strength. The LORD is my rock, my fortress, and my deliverer, my God, my rock in whom I take refuge, my shield, and the horn of my salvation, my stronghold."[28]

This psalm reminds us that God—through whom I was created and through whom I live and to whom I reach out when I complain and from whom I request all good things, because I know He is mine and that I should serve Him—this God is my helper in all good things, because I accomplish my good works through Him.

I also place my hope in God because His grace covers me like a good piece of clothing.

He gives us whatever we want when our good actions mirror His good intent. That's why every kindness we do has the sweetest aroma to God. Remember that in the Old Testament God was in no way pleased with the sacrificed blood of goats. Remember He spurned that sort of phony offering and demanded an authenticity of spirit from those who love Him. Remember how pleased God was with the genuine good will of those who said to Him, "We love you, God."

On Praising God

"Take delight in the LORD, and he will give you the desires of your heart."[29]

Angels are always delighting in God. With their voices and their lyres, they praise God's creation. We people on earth must also worship God, in two ways. First, we must praise Him, and, second, we must do good works.

God is known by our praise, while His miracles are seen in our acts of kindness, when we're filled with His love and are happy to be diligent in doing the Lord's work. All of God's miracles are accomplished through our praise and through our kindnesses.

What does this psalm teach us? Everyone who believes in God and who does good works for Him day in and day out must experience and give in to the joy of virtue. Be happy in the One who is Lord of the universe. Continue to follow Him. Love your Creator. After you become happy in God, He'll give you everything good. Life. Whatever you're looking for. Whatever your heart most wants, He'll give to you. Your trust in God will permit only good, healthy things to search you out.

Meditating on God will teach you spiritual confidence and how to pursue what pleases God. Talk to God, and don't forget to cry out to Him on behalf of your needy brother and sister. Then the aroma of good deeds—through God's love in you—will rise, and God will never stop fulfilling the requests you make out of concern for others. An intelligent person pays attention to these things and remembers them well.

Nature's Complaint Against Humanity

Then I heard air, earth, water, and fire complain to the tall cosmic man who wore the wind and earth's greenness:

> We can no longer do what God ordained us to do. We want to finish the journey He gave us, but we can't. We would run like we were meant to, if we could. But humans mistreat us. They abuse us. That's why we smell so horribly. That's why we're black with pollution and teeming with plagues. Is there no justice in the world? No order?

The cosmic man said:

> I'll cleanse you with My broom. I'll also put humanity on trial, until they repent. And they will. Whenever you're contaminated, I'll cleanse you by punishing those who pollute you. Can anyone belittle Me? See? When people don't follow My teachings and learn to speak with divine honesty, then the air (like the breath accompanying their unholy words) is bad. Greenness also withers

when humans pervert my teachings, saying, "How can we know a Lord we've never seen?"

But I say to them, "Don't you see Me day and night? Don't you see Me when you plant your crops, and when your seeds are nurtured by rainwater? All of creation has an affinity for its Creator and knows that one Person made it. Only people rebel. Seek God in the books His wisdom made, and get reacquainted with your Creator.

The Zither of Love

Heaven's my home, and God's love is my desire. I will seek to yearn for my Creator above all things. My greatest wish is to do what You ask me, God. Give me wings of determination and kindness, so I can soar above the stars of heaven, doing Your good will. You and Your holiness are all I need. Make me Your zither of love!

–7–

The Book of Divine Works

Some people hesitate to read Hildegard's books
because they don't like her perplexing, idiosyncratic style.
What they don't understand is that
it proves her prophecy is genuine.
—Gebeno, Prior of Eberbach,
Mirror of Future Times[30]

INTRODUCTION TO *THE BOOK OF DIVINE WORKS*

LIKE *SCIVIAS*, *The Book of Divine Works* took Hildegard a decade to finish. She was an old woman when she finished it in 1173—at seventy-five. In all, she spent some twenty-five years writing her three books on God. Some call *The Book of Divine Works* her best, most mature visionary creation. It presents ten visions in three parts: God's love for the world He single-handedly created, humanity's unique responsibilities and future judgment, and salvation history.

Vision four of book one, the very center of this final theological work, is a commentary on the prologue of John's Gospel. It is interesting that in her last major work Hildegard turns to this Gospel passage from John, which—for all its beauty and profundity—is a difficult text to analyze and explain. The tenth-century English Benedictine monk and seasoned sermon-writer Ælfric also wrote a splendid homiletic interpretation of this demanding text—and, like Hildegard, not until his later years. Perhaps maturity and an experienced eye are required to penetrate the heart of John's poetic Gospel and explain it to others. Hildegard may also have decided to analyze this Gospel passage critically as a way of claiming it for orthodox Christians and of dislodging it from the Cathars, who often quoted John to support their unorthodox anti-matter ideology.

As seen in the "Responsory for St. Disibod" in this reader, Hildegard understood the symbiotic relationship between body and soul. She knew that when the body and soul are not in sync, a person's whole world is out of whack. While she believed that the physical body is easily wayward and must be controlled, she did not teach that the body is evil. She did not malign the body the way the Cathars did. Hildegard's work also emphasizes taking care of the body, because it is the sacred temple of the Holy Spirit.

In other words, Hildegard understood that the body and the soul need to live together harmoniously, in God, and that true happiness results only when this balance is achieved. This is a favorite theme of the early Fathers of the Church. Ælfric, who frequently quoted from the early Church Fathers, reiterates that those who invite the Trinity to live with them will be *"gesælig"* (literally "soulful," and meaning "happy").

The Vision Preceding the Writing of
The Book of Divine Works

Later on, I saw a vision so full of Mystery it made me shiver. I grew numb from the wonder of it, and this drove my mind into a new dimension. Then God sent down a rain of understanding, and my soul knew the sweetness of the rich visions that John the Gospelist suckled at Jesus' breast. I understood then that this bright insight would inform some work not yet shown to me and that my writing would be renewed by it. I also knew that this book would explore the divine unknowable nature of all Creation.

Creation is mystery. The wind is made of air that stirs the sea, and condensation results, making rivers flow; and these rivers water the earth and give it vitality, just as a person's crisscrossing veins course through the body and strengthen it. The soul is made of air like the wind and helps each person do what's right. Just as airy breezes help fruit grow, the Holy Spirit is an air that floods a person's thoughts like a river, giving them wise discernment.

The Message

A voice from heaven sang out, saying to me:

Depressed child of God and daughter of much hard work, even though you've been thoroughly seared—so to speak—by endless terrible pains in your body, the deep mysteries of God have completely infused you. Give others an accurate account of what you see with your inner eye and what you hear with your soul's inner ear. Your testimony will benefit others. As a result, men and women will learn how to get to know their Creator, and they'll no longer refuse to adore God with excellence and respect.

That voice made me—heartbroken and fragile creature that I am—begin to write with a trembling hand, even though I was traumatized by more illnesses than I could count. As I started this task, I looked to the true and living Light and asked, "What should I write down?" I was never in a condition similar to sleep, nor was I in a spiritual ecstasy. I saw the visions with the inner eye of my spirit and grasped them with my inner ear.

The Beginning

In principio erat Verbum.
In the beginning was the Word.

This verse means this. I, the One with no beginning and from Whom every beginning begins; I, the Ancient of Days, assert that I am—all by Myself—day. I'm the day that's not lit by the sun. I'm the One who does the lighting of that orb. I'm also the Reason you cannot begin to fathom. My voice is thunder, and it moves the universe by creative sound. I did this.

On my Word, in Me limitless, I sparked a bright light through which countless angels flew, but they flashed away from me, forgetting their Creator. They forgot they were not God. God is singular, none other.

Later, I spoke humanity alive. I made man and woman within Me, and they are like Me. I knew one day My Son would wear humanity, too. Using My reason, I did all of this spiritually, and that's why you can see Me in humanity. This is similar to the way that the human spirit grasps a thing's essence through its name, and a thing's multiplicity through its number.

On Being Too Busy

If we get busy with something that isn't God's business, we feel God turns away from us. When we are preoccupied with ourselves, we fall under the influence of Satan's angels. But whenever we regret our wrong steps and our too-busy ways, and pray, "Help us, God!" He sends angels to protect us. They fly to our aid. Satan can't bother us then.

Ask God for good, really crave it, and He'll give you Milk from heaven. Gently at first, but later it will stream your way. Rivers of grace will strengthen you in every virtue. Those streams will continue to flow, increasing your integrity, until the day you die. You'll find God continuously renews you. All you have to do is ask Him.

Don't forget that God is balanced in all things. He isn't one way too-much-this or the other way too-much-that. No. Although He has absolute authority in everything, He never loses His sense of balance. He is never rude. If we listen to our good conscience, we, too, will be like God in kindness to others.

On the Holy Spirit

I am the ultimate fiery force igniting every spark of life. My breath knows nothing of death. I see you as you are and I judge you. I fly through the most distant galaxies of space on wings of wisdom, creating order wherever I go. I'm the divine flame of life, I burn above the golden fields, I sparkle on water, and I shine like the sun, the moon, and all the stars. Together with the loving, hidden power of the wind, I make everything come alive.

Remember that I'm also Reason. I inform the wind of the first Word that created all things. I'm your breath, I'm the breath of all things, and none die because I am that Life.

On Man and Woman

Man is the highest of God's creation, because he was made in God's image to praise and teach divine love, and because God appointed him the steward of all other creatures. But man needed a partner who was made like him. That's why God created woman, his spitting image. In woman, every single person who was born or will ever be born is hidden. Also, through God's strength, humanity was and is delivered through woman, with the same infinite power used to make the first man.

Men and women complement each other then. They empower each other. Man can't be "man" without woman, and woman can't be "woman" without man. They need each other to exist. Women strengthen men, and men console women. Also, man reveals the divine nature of God's Son, and woman His human nature.

On the Soul's Power

I saw the figure of a human in the middle of a shining wheel. The crown of this person's head touched the top of that wheel, the soles of his feet touched its bottom, and, his arms fully extended, the fingertips of his two hands touched the circle on both sides.

This vision means that humanity is at the center of the world, because humans are stronger than any other creature God made. How? Although physically small, people are powerful in their souls. The head of the soul looks up, while its feet are planted on solid ground. The soul can put into motion both exalted and common things. Whatever it does echoes through the universe, because its inner humanity has the power to accomplish such amazingly kind things.

A person's physical body is bigger than their literal heart, just as the soul is stronger than the body. This is what I mean: A person's heart lies hidden within their body, just as the physical body is surrounded by and hidden in the soul's powers, which cover the entire globe. Your body is in your soul, not your soul in your body. That's how you exist in God's knowledge and why you're able to do your best for God spiritually and also in worldly matters.

Those who are faithful always remember to turn to God, whether they succeed in what they're doing or fail. They know they always need Him. By focusing on God, they praise Him and respect Him. When you look with your physical eyes, you can see all the creatures on this earth. Looking with the eyes of faith, you're confident that you'll see the Lord, and we do see God in every creature, because we know He's the Creator of the whole world.

A Good Conscience

Each of us has a good conscience that supports God by stepping on our lusts. Our conscience removes everything that's dangerous and greedy in our souls. The right hand of the Lord accomplishes this so we can know God and carry out our daily work with respect for our Lord.

This right hand also raises me up in my repentance, even though I had been buried in a swamp of my own shortcomings. After I confess my sins, this hand creates the power of virtue that sparks within me such a love of God and such longing that I can never have too much of it. That's why I won't die in my sins if I turn to God and repent now. No, godly shame has much value and will help me live forever. It leads me to humility, and *humility* is another way of saying, "I'm sorry, God."

First—because we fear God and hell's punishments—we swerve to the left, and then—because we love God—we climb up to the right, because we hunger for the blessings of heaven. As we go along this path, we cultivate a good conscience, and this is the strongest armor we can wear. The right eye of good conscience looks all around it and decides that lusting for worldly pleasures has absolutely no value and is in fact boring. Honesty prefers to look at the light of truth instead.

On Not Complaining

"Do all that has to be done, and don't complain, either."[31]

Humanity stands at a crossroads today. If we search in God's Light for salvation and healing, we'll obviously receive it, but, as the Apostle Paul says in his letter to the Philippians quoted above, we mustn't fret and moan and whine and bellyache and grumble and grouse. If we stop complaining and don't sin, we'll become complete in our human nature.

Don't argue, either. Show your loyalty to God instead. If you're kind and don't harm anyone, you'll live a life free of bitterness. You'll live as God's children in the simplicity and joy of your good actions.

The Living Fountain

I am Love. I'm the Light of God, who is very much alive. Wisdom works through Me, and Humility, My partner, is rooted in the living Fountain. Humility is best friends with Peace. Through My living Light, the angels sparkle, because—as a ray of sunshine needs the sun—they need My brilliance.

You have seen objects and people reflected in water. In this same way, humanity is My reflection, because I'm the living Fountain. I am God's Spirit, and God Himself sends Me in all different directions, to give life to all things. There's no creature who can actually see life itself, no matter how hard you or anyone else may look for it, but you can feel your soul move. Water makes whatever is in it move, just as the soul makes the body move. Both flow.

Wisdom is what orders all things. Wisdom absorbed the words of the Old Testament prophets, of other wise men, and also of the Gospelists, and communicated them to Christ's disciples so that streams of living Water could flow around the world and, like a net, catch men and women in their grace. The water of the living Fountain sparkles with God's integrity.

The Signs of the End Times

There will be no justice then, because the greenness of virtue will have withered. The freshness of the earth will also dry up, because the atmosphere will no longer be pure, as it was originally. Summers will become cold, and winters will be hot. The Son said to His Father, "In the beginning, Creation was green. It flowered." That was a virile time, but now we live in a time of womanly infirmity, because everyone does only as they please. No one does what is right, and the Church is abandoned, like a widow who has lost the companionship of her husband, who once protected her and helped her.

Instead, evil clergy prostitute themselves for money. They're a stumbling block for My flock. They keep My little ones in the valleys and don't help them climb up the mountains. Their main goal is to accumulate money. They want diamond rings and other riches. They're greedy wolves who follow sheep tracks, killing those they can and scattering those they can't catch.

Hildegard's Acknowledgments

While working on this book, I was much encouraged and assisted by Volmar, a monk who truly followed St. Benedict's *Rule*. I was grief-stricken when he died. He was a happy man, and he helped me in so many ways. He served God by listening to every word of this vision, and he corrected them all and made them more orderly. He always kept me going.

He cautioned me never to stop writing because of my physical weaknesses and illnesses, but to persevere in setting down this vision. He served God until the day he died, always supporting me. I mourned him, saying: "Your will has now been done with this man, your servant, whom You gave me to help with these visions. Show me how to carry on!"

Abbot Ludwig of St. Eucharius in Trier stepped up next. He's a wise man, and it proved valuable that he was familiar with Volmar and my visions. Provost Wezelin of St. Andrew's in Cologne also came to my aid. His main desire was to do good works for God. These and other perspicacious men both consoled me and offered practical help with this book. Wezelin listened to the words of this vision without getting weary, finding them sweeter than honey.

That's how this book came to be—through God's grace and the help of many holy men. And I heard the living Light (Author of these visions) say, "I'll also reward Volmar and these other monks who helped in the making of this book."

CONCLUSION

EADSTRONG AND HUMBLE, annoying and comforting, Hildegard was real. She listened to God and followed Him by serving others. In the male-dominated world of the twelfth century—and in any world, in any century—this is the *sina qua non*, the one essential for living the abundant life of compassion. Hildegard makes this point in one of her many letters:

> Walk through the valley of humility and know peace. Lose your titanic, hard-to-satisfy ego. A greedy self-esteem is just a steep mountain you'll find dangerous to climb. It's also tricky (if not impossible) to come down from such heights, and anyhow the summit is too small for community. Focus on Love's splendid garden instead. Gather the flowers of humility and simplicity of soul. Study God's patience. Keep your eyes open. Decide to seek the all-powerful God with sincerity of mind.

Though separated by nine centuries, Hildegard's times and ours have much in common. Hers saw the rocky rise of nation-states—ours knows the turbulence of globalization versus nationalism. She watched men march off to so-called "holy" war—we witness similar manic religious fervor, manifesting itself worldwide in intolerance and in violence reminiscent of medieval crusades. Like her, we hear of self-pandering politicians, ecclesiastical indulgences, bribery, and clergies worthy of reform, only now God's name is used with the blinding speed of TV and of the Internet to shamelessly solicit the big bucks of the lowest form of green, which is greed.

Every generation also hatches and re-hashes pernicious old doctrines to sidetrack the human heart. Today we find our modern world wandering in the dim dualism of body and spirit. The body as the temple of the Holy Spirit is forgotten, and worse, the body is often viewed as a spiritual nuisance. As John O'Donohue says in *Anam Cara*, "The body is much sinned against, even in a religion based on the Incarnation."[32] Even the earth's "body" is ignored. We forget to look at the shining stars above our heads at night, because we suffer from spiritual amnesia. We're too "busy" to notice the beauty of God's creation and our responsibility for its care. Our current ecological crises tragically reflect this, as does our inability to stay happy for very long. Hildegard is a tonic for us, because she fills Catharism's dualistic rejection of the body, sexuality, marriage, the Trinity, and the Eucharist, with God's goodness and the essential wholeness of a divine creation that refuses to be separated into neat-but-useless categories of earth and spirit, body and soul, nature and people.

Thankfully, when we read Hildegard, we get this Whole, not parts. Metaphors come to life in strange and wonderful ways. Her work shows us that, within us, the Incarnation lives, Spring greens, Light shines, Music sings, Bread sustains, Words instruct, and—even though dark, avaricious Wolves prowl—Stars are bright and Love heals. Reading Hildegard, you can always expect contact with the ordinary ways of Mystery. Meeting God in her work, we find our expectations change, for the kinder. For the more merciful.

ACKNOWLEDGMENTS

SPECIAL THANKS GO TO President Harold E. Newman and to Provost L. Craig Shull of Shorter College for sustaining this book through the Scholar-in-Residence position. I'm also indebted to interim Provost H. William "Bill" Rice in ways vaster than the Montana sky. Wilson Hall's joy for Hildegard sparked many discussions in a conversation that is now decades-long, while Renva Watterson's excellence as a communicator and administrator and her sisterly support kept me going. Special thanks also go to Dick Taylor for helping my family transition to Korea and back. Melissa Tarrant and Gary Davis helped by explaining the painful and unique phenomena of migraines to me.

Jon Sweeney and Lil Copan at Paraclete Press are synonymous with high editorial standards, and phone, e-mail, and real-time conversations with them shaped this book. Special thanks go to Jon Sweeney for cutting the original manuscript wisely and for suggesting additions where needed. Robert Edmonson has been a modern day Volmar to this book; nothing escaped his wholesome vision, and for his conscientious diligence, I am profoundly grateful. I'm also thankful to the entire community at Paraclete Press for their excellent assistance, including Pamela Jordan, Sister Mercy, Carol Showalter, Danielle Bushnell, Karen Minster, Rachel McKendree, Jennifer Lynch, Sarah Andre, and Sister Antonia.

Hildegard would understand if I praised my first grammar teacher, Dot Whitfield, for making me fall in love with diagramming. John Algeo deserves a special nod for advising me nearly two decades ago to make my translations "smooth-reading in Modern English and faithful to both the sense and the form of the original." Daily conversations with Mary Lee Chubbs nourished this book, and my former students Danielle Buckley and Ben McFry helped by questioning everything. Karen S. Price made this and every book possible through her wise Rolfing in Palo Alto; it is fitting that I thank her in this particular book, because Karen is as brave as Hildegard ever was.

Thanks are also given to Sister Mary Tewes at Walburg Monastery in Covington, Kentucky, for warm e-mails connecting me to the heart of Benedictine life; to Shorter College librarians, Dean Kimmetha "Kim" Herndon, Bettie Sumner, John Rivest, and DeWayne Williams, for sharing their brilliance; to my parents, Loren and Doris Acevedo, for turning-up; and to Lucky for keeping me company.

I'm most thankful to my family. My husband created the splendid map of Hildegard's Germany. Thank you, Sean, for doing that in between fixing bathroom leaks, sistering joists, bricking walls, adjusting negative grade, and laying beautiful Tuscan tile. To Kate and John, again, thank you for being patient with your sometimes daft mom. I love you.

CHRONOLOGY *of* HILDEGARD'S LIFE

BEFORE HILDEGARD'S BIRTH

1056–1106. Henry IV is King of Germany, and he is Emperor from 1084–1106. Hildegard once called him "a worshipper of Baal," and in her letter-sermon to Abbot Helengerus (see the "Letters" section), the unnamed "dictator" is probably Henry IV.

1073. Gregory VII becomes Pope and leads the Church until his death in 1085. He legislated the Gregorian Decrees against simony, investiture, and clerical marriage.

1076. Pope Gregory VII excommunicates Henry IV.

1080. Henry IV appoints the Anti-pope Clement III, who promotes simony, anti-celibacy, and the pro-clerical concubinage party.

1086. Victor III becomes Pope and leads the Church until his death the next year.

1088. Urban II is elected Pope and leads the Church until his death in 1099.

1095. At the Synod of Clermont in France, Pope Urban II begins the Crusades by calling for an attack against the Muslim world.

1096–99. The first crusade is waged.

HILDEGARD'S BIRTH AND EARLY YEARS

Summer AD 1098. The tenth and last child of Hildebert and Mechthild, Hildegard is born in Bermersheim, near Mainz, in the area of western Germany called *Rheinhessen*.

1099. Jerusalem is taken, and then the Crusaders massacre nearly everyone there.

1100. The Anti-pope Clement III dies.

1106. As a young child, Hildegard is dedicated as a tithe to the Church. Henry IV dies.

1112. On All Saints' Day (November 1st), Hildegard enters the hermitage of the aristocratic Jutta of Spanheim, a high-born recluse attached to the monastery of Disibodenberg.

THE DEATH OF JUTTA AND THE BEGINNING OF *SCIVIAS*

1136. Jutta dies. With the passing of time, the hermitage has grown into a small Benedictine convent, and its nuns elect Hildegard as their abbess.

1140s. The Catharist religious movement begins in Germany. Hildegard will fight this Gnostic Christian sect's anti-Trinity, anti-Eucharistic, anti-marriage theology in her works.

1141. Hildegard has a fiery vision commanding her to write down her revelations. This is the beginning of *Scivias*, her first major theological work, which takes Hildegard ten years to complete.

1145. The friend and student of Bernard of Clairvaux, Abbot Bernardo Pignatelli, becomes Pope Eugenius III (until 1153).

HILDEGARD'S PAPAL APPROVAL AND THE SECOND CRUSADE

1147. Hildegard writes the Cistercian Bernard of Clairvaux, asking the Church to validate her visions. Soon after, Pope Eugenius III reads from the unfinished *Scivias* manuscript at a reform synod in nearby Trier, and it is enthusiastically received by the assembled clergymen and dignitaries. The Pope immediately authorizes Hildegard's writings. This year also marks the real beginning of Hildegard's three decades of letter-writing.

1147–49. The second crusade occurs. Conrad III of Germany and Louis VII of France march to Asia Minor but do not win any major battles.

1148. Hildegard is already well-known for her musical compositions. These will be collected later in the *Symphonia*. She is also busy writing letters to secular and religious leaders and laypeople.

THE FOUNDING OF RUPERTSBERG AND THE COMPLETION OF *SCIVIAS*

1150. After much opposition from the Disibodenberg monks, Hildegard founds her first abbey nineteen miles northeast of Disibodenberg at Rupertsberg. The Rupertsberg convent was burned during the Thirty Years War in 1632.

1151. Hildegard completes *Scivias*, ten years after starting it. She also finishes an early version of the first extant morality play, *The Play of the Virtues*. It is sometimes also called the first creation of musical theater or opera. Hildegard's *Play of the Virtues* was probably composed for the 1152 dedication of the Rupertsberg convent. Hildegard revised this lyrical drama well into her later years. Her favorite assistant, nun Richardis of Stade, is asked to lead another convent at Bassum in Lower Saxony, near Bremen, quite a distance to the north. Hildegard is distraught at her close friend's departure, which she had vigorously opposed. Hildegard also wrote her *Lingua ignota*, a secret language that she probably envisioned as being used by the sisters in her community.

1151–58. Hildegard continues writing letters, liturgical songs, and music. She also writes the *Physica* and *Causes and Cures*.

1152. On March 4th, Frederick Barbarossa is elected king of Germany. On May 1st, Hildegard dedicates her new convent at Rupertsberg. Her nuns may have performed *The Play of the Virtues* for this occasion. On October 29th, Richardis dies, not long after her move to Bassum.

1153. Pope Eugenius dies on July 8th, and St. Bernard of Clairvaux dies on August 21st. Anastasius IV becomes pope on July 9th, and leads the Church until his death less than a year and a half later.

1154. Henry II becomes King of England (until 1189). His wife is Eleanor of Aquitaine (see the "Letters" section of this book). Pope Anastasius IV dies on December 3rd, and the Englishman Nicholas Breakspear becomes Pope Adrian IV (until 1159).

SYMPHONIA, PHYSICA, CAUSES AND CURES, AND MORE LETTERS

1155. A version exists of Hildegard's *Symphonia*, indicating that this remarkable text was published sometime before this year. Frederick Barbarossa is crowned Holy Roman Emperor on June 18th, and Hildegard meets him around this time when he invites her to his palace at Ingelheim. She must have impressed him, because later he grants the Rupertsberg convent an edict of imperial protection in perpetuity, and whenever he orders attacks on certain monasteries supporting the Roman pope, Hildegard's convent is always spared. Abbot Kuno of St. Disibod dies this year.

1157. Bonn-born Elisabeth of Schönau is made abbess of the nuns in her community, under the Abbot Hildelin.

1158–62. Hildegard says these were years of constant ill health for her. She seems to have spent many years suffering from recurring fevers, exhaustion, and breathing trouble.

THE BOOK OF LIFE'S MERITS AND THREE OF FOUR PREACHING TOURS

1158–63. Hildegard writes her second visionary work, *The Book of Life's Merits*.

1158. Despite poor health, her busy ministry as abbess, and the writing of *The Book of Life's Merits*, sixty-year-old Hildegard launches the first of four preaching tours, traveling along the River Main, from Mainz east to Bamberg, also stopping at Wertheim, Würzburg, Kitzingen, and Ebrach. These extensive preaching tours, unheard of at that time for a woman, would have been arduous. Even with some possible boat trips, they would have required Hildegard to travel much by land. She preached at monasteries as well as publicly.

1159–76. Pope Alexander III is elected, and the eighteen-year schism between the Church and Emperor Barbarossa occurs. When Barbarossa backs the Anti-pope Victor IV (1159–64), Pope Alexander excommunicates the Emperor in 1160. Barbarossa will support two more anti-popes, Paschalis III (1164–68) and Calixtus III (1168–78).

1160. Hildegard begins her second preaching tour, traveling along the Rhine River from Trier south to Metz, also stopping at the monastic community in Krauftal. On Pentecost, she makes a public appearance at Trier.

1161. Hildegard begins her third preaching tour, traveling for a second time along the Rhine River, from Boppard north to Cologne and Werden, including stops at Andernach and Siegburg. At Cologne she preaches to both the clergy and laypeople.

THE *BOOK OF DIVINE WORKS* AND THE FOUNDING OF EIBINGEN

1163–73/74. Hildegard takes some ten years to write the *The Book of Divine Works*, her third major visionary work. She also writes to the Emperor, but without taking sides in the schism (this time).

1164. Hildegard writes again to the Emperor, to express her disapproval of his appointment of Anti-pope Paschalis III.

1165. Hildegard founds her second convent at Eibingen, high above the town of Rüdesheim, and across the Rhine from her convent at Rupertsberg. She begins crossing the Rhine River twice a week to visit those under her care at Eibingen. The contemporary St. Hildegard's Abbey, built between 1900 and 1904, stands on the site of the medieval Eibingen convent.

1167–70. Hildegard experiences more years of chronic bad health.

1168. Hildegard writes the Emperor to warn him of God's disapproval of his appointment of Anti-pope Callistus III.

AN EXORCISM, TWO *VITAS*, AND THE LAST PREACHING TOUR

1170. Hildegard works as an exorcist to cure from demonic possession a noble Cologne woman named Sigewize, then accepts her into the community. Hildegard writes the *Life of Saint Disibod* and the *Life of Saint Rupert*, and begins her fourth and last preaching tour, this time in Swabia, heading south and stopping at Maulbronn, Hirsau, Kirchheim, and Zwiefalten. Thomas Becket is murdered at Canterbury Cathedral.

1173. Hildegard's confidant, secretary, and long-time friend Volmar dies.

1173/74. Hildegard finishes *The Book of Divine Works* some ten years after commencing it.

1174. Godfrey comes to Rupertsberg from Disibodenberg, and, as Volmar's successor, he starts writing Hildegard's *Vita*.

1176. Godfrey dies, having finished only one book of Hildegard's *Vita*.

1177. The Belgian monk Guibert of Gembloux becomes Hildegard's secretary.

DISAGREEMENT WITH THE MAINZ CLERGY AND HILDEGARD'S DEATH

1178. Hildegard finds herself in conflict with the Mainz clergy over a man they consider excommunicated and she considers pardoned. The Mainz clergy issue an interdict against the convent of Rupertsberg, forbidding Hildegard's community from celebrating mass and allowing the divine office to be performed only in whispers.

1179. Archbishop Christian of Mainz lifts the ban on the Rupertsberg community in March.

17 September 1179. Hildegard dies at Rupertsberg. She is eighty-one.

AFTER HILDEGARD'S DEATH

c. 1186. Theoderic of Echternach finishes the *Vita* for Hildegard that Godfrey had started in 1174. Theodoric is responsible for the second and third books, as well as the prefaces.

1187. The Kurd Saladin, Sultan of Egypt, recaptures Jerusalem, and Pope Gregory VIII calls for a third Crusade.

1190. During the third Crusade, Barbarossa drowns on June 10th, crossing the Saleph River in the Roman province of Cilicia, which is part of modern Turkey.

1200s–1300s. Attempts to canonize Hildegard fail for reasons not clear, but her name is added to the *Roman Martyrology* in the sixteenth century, guaranteeing her sainthood.[33] As Sister Judith Sutera explains:

> For the first centuries, the "naming" and veneration of saints was an informal process, occurring locally and operating locally.
> . . . When they began to codify, between the thirteenth and six-teenth centuries, they did not go back and apply any official process to those persons who were already widely recognized and venerated. They simply "grandfathered in" anyone whose cult had been flourishing for 100 years or more. So many quite famous, ancient, and even non-existent saints who have had feast days and devotions since the apostolic era were never canonized per se.[34]

1997/98. Jubilee Year commemorates the 900th birthday of St. Hildegard.

FURTHER READING MATERIAL
and RECORDINGS *of*
HILDEGARD'S MUSIC

CRITICAL EDITIONS OF HILDEGARD'S LATIN TEXTS

Corpus Christianorum Continuatio Medievalis (CCCM) began publishing critical editions of Latin patristic and other texts in 1966, and to date it has published over 200 of these, with some eight to ten new titles appearing each year. For more information, see the website that Brepols Publishers maintains at http://www.corpuschristianorum.org/series/cccm.html. Some of the titles for Hildegard include the following:

Carlevaris, Angela, ed. *Liber vite meritorum* (*Hildegardis Bingensis*). CCCM 90. Turnhout, Belgium: Brepols, 1995.

Derolez, Albert, ed. Guibert of Gembloux, *Epistolae.* CCCM 66-66a. Turnhout, Belgium: Brepols, 1988, 1989.

Derolez, Albert, and Peter Dronke, eds. *Liber divinorum operum* (*Hildegardis Bingensis*). CCCM 92. Turnhout, Belgium: Brepols, 1996.

Führkötter, Adelgundis, and Angela Carlevaris, eds. *Scivias* (*Hildegardis Bingensis*). CCCM 43, 43A. Turnhout, Belgium: Brepols, 2003.

Kaiser, Paul, ed. *Causae et curae*. Leipzig: Teubner, 1903.

Klaes, Monika, ed. Gottfried of Disibodenberg and Theoderich of Echtenach, *Vita sanctae Hildegardis (Hildegardis Bingensis)*. CCCM 126. Turnhout, Belgium: Brepols, 1993.

Migne, Jacques Paul, ed. *Sanctae Hildegardis Abbatissae Opera Omnia* in *Patrologia Latina*. Volume 197, cols. 383–738. Paris: Migne, 1855.

Pitra, Jean-Baptiste, ed. *Analecta Sanctae Hildegardis Opera. Analecta Sacra*, vol. 8. Monte Cassino: Typis Sacri Montis Casinensis, 1882.

Van Acker, Lieven, ed. *Epistolarium I (I-XC) (Hildegardis Bingensis)*. CCCM 91. Turnhout, Belgium: Brepols, 1991.

———, ed. *Epistolarium II (XCI-CCLr.) (Hildegardis Bingensis)*. CCCM 91A. Turnhout, Belgium: Brepols, 1993.

SELECTED ENGLISH TRANSLATIONS OF HILDEGARD

Atherton, Mark, trans. *Hildegard of Bingen: Selected Writings*. London: Penguin, 2001.

Baird, Joseph L., and Radd K. Ehrman, trans. *The Letters of Hildegard of Bingen. Vol. I*. Oxford: Oxford University Press, 1994.

———, trans. *The Letters of Hildegard of Bingen. Vol. II*. Oxford: Oxford University Press, 1998.

———, trans. *The Letters of Hildegard of Bingen. Vol. III*. Oxford: Oxford University Press, 2004.

Bowie, Fiona, and Oliver Davies, eds. *Hildegard of Bingen: An Anthology*. London: SPCK, 1990.

Dronke, Peter, ed. and trans. *Ordo virtutum, The Play of the Virtues*. In *Nine Medieval Latin Plays*, 147–84. Cambridge: Cambridge University Press, 1994.

Feiss, Hugh, trans. *Explanation of the Rule of St. Benedict by Hildegard of Bingen.* Peregrina Translation Series. 1990. Toronto: Peregrina, 1996.

——, trans. *The Life of Hildegard of Bingen by Gottfried of Disibodenberg and Theodoric of Echternach.* Peregrina Translation Series. Toronto: Peregrina, 1996.

Flanagan, Sabina, trans. *Secrets of God: Writings of Hildegard of Bingen.* Boston: Shambhala Publications, Inc., 1996.

Fox, Matthew, ed. *Book of Divine Works, with Letters and Songs.* Trans. Robert Cunningham, et al. Santa Fe: Bear & Co., 1987.

Führkötter, Adelgundis, and James McGrath. *The Life of Holy Hildegard by the Monks Gottfried and Theodoric.* Collegeville, MN: The Liturgical Press, 1980.

Hart, Columba, and Jane Bishop, trans. *Scivias.* Classics of Western Spirituality. New York: Paulist Press, 1990.

Hozeski, Bruce W., trans. *The Book of the Rewards of Life (Liber vitae meritorum).* New York: Oxford University Press, 1997.

Newman, Barbara, ed. and trans. *Hildegard of Bingen: Symphonia: A Critical Edition of the Symphonia Armonie Celestium Revelationum.* Ithaca, NY: Cornell University Press, 1998.

Young, Abigail Ann. *Translations from Rupert, Hildegard, and Guibert of Gembloux.* 1999. [27 March 2006] http://www.chass.utoronto.ca/~young/trnintro.html

GENERAL COMMENTARY ON HILDEGARD

Burnett, Charles, and Peter Dronke, eds. *Hildegard of Bingen: The Context of Her Thought and Art.* The Warburg Colloquia. London: The University of London, 1998.

Cherewatuk, Karen, and Ulrike Wiethaus, eds. *Dear Sister: Medieval Women and the Epistolary Genre.* Middle Ages Series. Philadelphia: University of Pennsylvania Press, 1993.

Davidson, Audrey Ekdahl. *The Ordo Virtutum of Hildegard of Bingen: Critical Studies.* Kalamazoo, MI: Medieval Institute Publications, 1992.

Dronke, Peter. *Women Writers of the Middle Ages: A Critical Study of Texts from Perpetua to Marguerite Porete.* Cambridge: Cambridge University Press, 1984.

Flanagan, Sabina. *Hildegard of Bingen: A Visionary Life.* London: Routledge, 1998.

King-Lenzmeier, Anne H. *Hildegard of Bingen: An Integrated Vision.* Collegeville, MN: Liturgical Press, 2001.

Maddocks, Fiona. *Hildegard of Bingen: The Woman of Her Age.* New York: Image Books/Doubleday, 2003.

Newman, Barbara. *Sister of Wisdom: St. Hildegard's Theology of the Feminine.* Berkeley: University of California Press, 1987.

———, ed. *Voice of the Living Light: Hildegard of Bingen and Her World.* Berkeley: University of California, 1998.

Pernoud, Régine. *Hildegard of Bingen: Inspired Conscience of the Twelfth Century.* Translated by Paul Duggan. New York: Marlowe & Co., 1998.

Schipperges, Heinrich. *The World of Hildegard of Bingen: Her Life, Times, and Visions.* Translated by John Cumming. Collegeville, MN: The Liturgical Press, 1999.

Wilson, Katharine. *Medieval Women Writers.* Athens, GA: University of Georgia Press, 1984.

ON HILDEGARD'S ILLUMINATIONS

Fox, Matthew. *Illuminations of Hildegard of Bingen*. Santa Fe, NM: Bear & Company, 1985.

RECORDINGS OF HILDEGARD'S MUSIC (DISCOGRAPHY)

The early-music ensembles Sequentia and Sinfonye are steadily recording Hildegard's musical works.

900 Years: Hildegard von Bingen. Sequentia. Box Set (8 discs). RCA 77505, 1998.

11,000 Virgins: Chants for the Feast of St. Ursula. Anonymous 4, Harmonia Mundi 907200, 1997.

Aurora. Sinfonye, dir. Stevie Wishart. Vol. 2. Celestial Harmonies 13128, 1997.

The Emma Kirkby Collection. Christopher Page. Hyperion 66227, 1993.

A Feather on the Breath of God: Sequences and Hymns by Abbess Hildegard of Bingen. Gothic Voices, dir. Christopher Page, Emma Kirkby (soprano). Hyperion DCA 66039, 1981.

Gesänge der hl. Hildegard von Bingen. Schola der Benediktinerinnenabtei St. Hildegard, dir. M.-I. Ritscher. Bayer 100116, 1979.

Hildegard of Bingen: The Harmony of Heaven. Ellen Oak. Bison Publications 1, 1996.

Hildegard von Bingen: Canticles of Ecstasy. Sequentia, dir. Barbara Thornton. Deutsche Harmonia mundi 05472-77320-2, 1994.

Hildegard von Bingen: Heavenly Revelations. Oxford Camerata, dir. Jeremy Summerly. Naxos 8.550998, 1994.

Hildegard von Bingen und ihre Zeit: Geistliche Musik des 12. Ensemble für frühe Musik Augsburg. Christophorus 74584, 1990.

Jouissance. Viriditas, dir. Juliette Hughes. Spectrum/Cistercian Publications, ISBN 0-86786-344-7, 1993.

The Lauds of St. Ursula. Early Music Institute, dir. Thomas Binkley. Focus 911, 1991.

Monk and the Abbess: Music of Hildegard von Bingen and Meredith Monk. Musica Sacra, dir. Richard Westenburg. Catalyst 09026-68329-2, 1996.

O nobilissima viriditas. Catherine Schroeder, et al. Champeaux CSM 0006, 1995.

O nobilissima viriditas. Sinfonye, dir. Stevie Wishart. Vol. 3. Celestial Harmonies 13129, 2004.

Ordo virtutum. Sequentia, dir. Barbara Thornton. 2 disks. Deutsche Harmonia mundi 77051-2-RG, 1982.

Symphoniae: Geistliche Gesänge. Sequentia, dir. Barbara Thornton. Deutsche Harmonia mundi 770230-2-RG, 1983.

Symphoniae: Spiritual Songs. Sequentia. RCA 77020, 1993.

Symphony of the Harmony of Celestial Revelations. Sinfonye, dir. Stevie Wishart. Vol. 1. Celestial Harmonies 13127-2, 1996.

Unfurling Love's Creation: Chants by Hildegard von Bingen. Norma Gentile. Lyrichord Early Music Series (LEMS) 8027, 1997.

Voice of the Blood. Sequentia, dir. Barbara Thornton. 2 disks. Deutsche Harmonia mundi 05472-77346-2, 1995.

Other Background Reading

Barber, Richard. *Bestiary: MS Bodley 764.* Woodbridge, UK: Boydell Press, 1999.

Bynum, Caroline Walker. *Holy Feast and Holy Fast: The Religious Significance of Food to Medieval Women.* Berkeley: University of California Press, 1987.

———. *Resurrection of the Body in Western Christianity, 200–1336.* New York: Columbia University Press, 1995.

Constable, Giles Constable. *The Reformation of the Twelfth Century.* Cambridge: Cambridge University Press, 1998.

Dronke, Peter, ed. *A History of Twelfth-Century Western Philosophy.* Cambridge: Cambridge University Press, 1992.

Holweck, the Rt. Reverend Frederick G. *A Biographical Dictionary of the Saints, with a General Introduction on Hagiology.* 1924. Detroit: Omnigraphics, 1990.

Lachman, Barbara. *The Journal of Hildegard of Bingen: A Novel.* New York: Crown, 1993.

———. *Hildegard: The Last Year.* Boston: Shambhala, 1997.

McBrien, Richard. *Lives of the Saints: From Mary and St. Francis of Assisi to John XXIII and Mother Teresa.* San Francisco: HarperSanFrancisco, 2003.

O'Donohue, John. *Anam Cara.* New York: HarperCollins, 1998.

Ohanneson, Joan. *Scarlet Music. Hildegard of Bingen: A Novel.* New York: Crossroad Publishing Company, 1997.

Pelikan, Jaroslav. *Mary Through the Centuries: Her Place in the History of Culture.* New Haven: Yale University Press, 1996.

Sacks, Oliver. *Migraine: Understanding a Common Disorder.* 1985. Reprint. London: Vintage Books, 1999.

Santos Paz, José Carlos, ed. *La Obra de Gebenón de Eberbach.* Firenze: SISMEL-Edizioni del Galluzzo, 2004.

Sherman, Bernard D. "'Mistaking the Tail for the Comet': An Interview with Christopher Page on Hildegard of Bingen," 1999. [16 July 2006.] For the *All Music Guide* at www.allclassical.com. http://homepages.kdsi.net/~sherman/pageonhild.htm.

Silvas, Anna. *Jutta and Hildegard: The Biographical Sources.* University Park, PA: The Pennsylvania State University Press, 1998.

Ulrich, Ingeborg. *Hildegard of Bingen: Mystic, Healer, Companion of the Angels.* Translated by Linda M. Maloney. Collegeville, MN: Liturgical Press, 1993.

Ward, Benedicta. *Miracles and the Medieval Mind.* Philadelphia: University of Pennsylvania, 1987.

NOTES

1. Christopher Page, a Cambridge musicologist, is quoted by Bernard D. Sherman at http://homepages.kdsi.net/~sherman/pageonhild.htm. [16 July 2006.] See "'Mistaking the Tail for the Comet': An Interview with Christopher Page on Hildegard of Bingen," 1999, written for the All Music Guide.

2. Matthew Fox, *Illuminations of Hildegard of Bingen* (Santa Fe, NM: Bear & Company, 1985).

3. Barbara Newman, *Sister of Wisdom: St. Hildegard's Theology of the Feminine* (Berkeley: University of California Press, 1987), xvii.

4. Emphasis has been added here. See *Incandescence*, by Carmen Butcher, 95.

5. This famous quotation is from a letter Keats wrote to his brothers George and Thomas on Sunday, 21 December 1817. John Keats, *Selected Letters*, Robert Gittings, ed. Oxford World Classics, 2nd Rev. ed. (Oxford: Oxford University Press, 2002), 41.

6. 2 Corinthians 12:9.

7. See 1 Corinthians 14:34–35: "[W]omen should be silent in the churches. For they are not permitted to speak, but should be subordinate, as the law also says. If there is anything they desire to know, let them ask their husbands at home. For it is shameful for a woman to speak in church."

8. See Barbara Newman's *Sister of Wisdom*, 27.

9. Verses 1–6a.

10. Rachel M. Srubas, *Oblation: Meditations on St. Benedict's Rule* (Brewster, MA: Paraclete Press, 2006).

11. For more information on the *Symphonia* manuscripts and the order of their songs, see Barbara Newman's *Symphonia*, 51 ff. and 65 ff. The translations featured in this reader correspond, in the following order, to the songs included in Newman's *Symphonia*: The first number below represents the poem's place in this reader; then my title is given, followed in parentheses by Newman's corresponding number for the song, with her title for it: 1. "Life-Altering Love" (1, "Responsory for the Creator"); 2. "To Sophia" (2, "Antiphon for Divine Wisdom"); 3. "The Sheep, Listening" (4, "Antiphon for the Redeemer"); 4. "The Most Sanguine Moment" (5, "Antiphon for the Redeemer"); 5. "A Prayer from Poverty to Greatness" (6, "Antiphon for God the Father"); 6. "A Mystery of Mother and Maker" (10, "Antiphon for the Virgin"); 7. "The Open Invitation" (11, "Antiphon for the Virgin"); 8. "That a King Would Bow" (16, "Antiphon for the Virgin"); 9. "And a Woman Would Stand Up" (18, "Alleluia-verse for the Virgin"); 10. "Grateful for the Unobtrusive Good" (19, "Song to the Virgin"); 11. "The First Verb" (24, "Antiphon for the Holy Spirit"); 12. "The First Fire" (28, "Sequence for the Holy Spirit"); 13. "In Praise of Guardian Angels" (30, "Responsory for the Angels"); 14. "In Gratitude for Perspicacious Men" (31, "Antiphon for Patriarchs and Prophets"); 15. "The Apostles as the Voice of God's Son" (33, "Antiphon for the Apostles"); 16. "The Mighty Wildness of Service" (40, "Antiphon for Confessors"); 17. "In Praise of St. Disibod" (43, "Responsory for Saint Disibod"); 18. "In Praise of St. Rupert" (49, "Sequence for Saint Rupert"); 19. "At the Foundation of Goodness" (55, "Antiphon for Virgins"); 20. "A Monastic Prayer for Purity" (57, "Symphony of Virgins"); 21. "In Praise of St.

Ursula" (64, "Sequence for Saint Ursula"); 22, 23, 24. "Three Antiphons for Church Dedications" (66, 67, 68); 25. "The First Daylight" ("*O Verbum Patris*"); 26. "Mary's Love Song" ("*O Fili dilectissime*"); and 27. "The First Artist" ("*O factura Dei*").

12. The Latin *frumentum* for "corn, grain," is often translated, "wheat," but I chose the less well-known "spelt," an ancient form of wheat, because Hildegard knew it well and often writes about it. Spelt is making a comeback today in the diet of the health-conscious for its high fiber, abundant protein, and rich nutrients (particularly B-complex vitamins). Also, gluten-sensitive people find it easy to digest. Unfortunately, spelt is not a mainstream bread because its tough outer hull makes it more expensive to process into flour. Hildegard's holistic view of God's world paid special attention to dietary needs, and she viewed spelt not only as good for the body but also as beneficial for the soul. She called spelt "the best" of all grains and recommended it for breakfast. In Germany, spelt is the *Dinkel* in *Dinkelbrot*. The Abbey of St. Hildegard (situated above Rüdesheim and the Rhine River) makes spelt products today.

13. In this antiphon, Hildegard uses five words from her self-constructed language, the *Lingua ignota*, or "secret language"; this is the only recorded time that she did. The first, for "willowy" in line one, is *orzchis*. "Aroma" and "people's," in line three, are *caldemia* and *loifolum*, respectively. "Anointed" in line seven and "shining" in line eight are *crizanta* and *chorzta*. Little is known about the use of this "unknown tongue," but it has a strange alphabet of twenty-three characters, and its lexicon contains about 1000 neologisms, mostly nouns, hierarchically arranged, for God and angels, then words for humans and our family relationships, followed by nouns for things like parts of the body,

illnesses, days, months, clothing, household tools, plants, and a few birds. Perhaps Hildegard was thinking to create a language for her community that would be more nearly like communication in the Garden of Eden before the Fall.

14. Régine Pernoud, *Hildegard of Bingen: Inspired Conscience of the Twelfth Century*, translated by Paul Duggan (New York: Marlowe & Co., 1998), viii.

15. Proverbs 10:4.

16. Song of Solomon 8:1.

17. C. S. Lewis, *The Great Divorce* (New York: Touchstone Book, 1996), 105.

18. Psalm 118:9.

19. The Right Reverend Frederick G. Holweck, *A Biographical Dictionary of the Saints, with a General Introduction on Hagiology*, 1924 (Detroit: Omnigraphics, 1990), 485.

20. See 1 Timothy 2:9.

21. Matthew 19:6.

22. Both Adelheid and the younger Richardis had decided to leave Hildegard's community to become abbesses, a decision Hildegard passionately opposed, as this letter shows.

23. Song of Solomon 2:12.

24. Psalm 94:12.

25. Song of Solomon 2:12.

26. Psalm 150:3, 6.

27. See Ezekiel 1:10, Revelation 4:7.

28. Psalm 18:1–2.

29. Psalm 37:4.

30. This quotation comes from Gebeno's *Speculum futurorum temporum sive Pentachronon sancte Hildegardis* (*Mirror of Future Times*

or the Five Ages), compiled in 1220. This widely disseminated condensed version of Hildegard's apocalyptic visions was largely responsible for keeping her name alive at that time. No edited *Pentachronon* exists yet, but excerpts are found in Jean-Baptiste Pitra's *Analecta Sanctae Hildegardis*, volume 8 of *Analecta Sacra* (Monte Cassino: Typis Sacri Montis Casinensis, 1882), 483–488.

31. Compare Philippians 2:14.
32. John O'Donohue, *Anam Cara* (New York: HarperCollins, 1998), 46.
33. Sabina Flanagan, *Hildegard of Bingen: A Visionary Life* (London: Routledge, 1998), 11–12, and Fiona Maddocks, *Hildegard of Bingen: The Woman of Her Age* (New York: Image Books/Doubleday, 2003), 254 ff. The story of Hildegard's sainthood is complex, fascinating, and fraught with questions.
34. This quotation comes from an August 23, 2006 e-mail sent to me by Sister Judith Sutera. Sister Deborah Harmeling was also helpful in increasing my understanding of this byzantine topic.

About Paraclete Press

Who We Are

Paraclete Press is an ecumenical publisher of books and recordings on Christian spirituality. Our publishing represents a full expression of Christian belief and practice—from Catholic to Evangelical, from Protestant to Orthodox.

Paraclete Press is the publishing arm of the Community of Jesus, an ecumenical monastic community in the Benedictine tradition. As such, we are uniquely positioned in the marketplace without connection to a large corporation and with informal relationships to many branches and denominations of faith.

We like it best when people buy our books from booksellers, our partners in successfully reaching as wide an audience as possible.

What We Are Doing

Books

Paraclete Press publishes books that show the richness and depth of what it means to be Christian. Although Benedictine spirituality is at the heart of all that we do, we publish books that reflect the Christian experience across many cultures, time periods, and houses of worship.

We publish books that nourish the vibrant life of the church and its people—books about spiritual practice, formation, history, ideas, and customs.

We have several different series of books within Paraclete Press, including the bestselling Living Library series of modernized classic texts; A Voice from the Monastery—giving voice to men and women monastics about what it means to live a spiritual life today; award-winning literary faith fiction; and books that explore Judaism and Islam and discover how these faiths inform Christian thought and practice.

Recordings

From Gregorian chant to contemporary American choral works, our music recordings celebrate the richness of sacred choral music through the centuries. Paraclete is proud to distribute the recordings of the internationally acclaimed choir Gloriæ Dei Cantores, who have been praised for their "rapt and fathomless spiritual intensity" by *American Record Guide,* and the Gloriæ Dei Cantores Schola, which specializes in the study and performance of Gregorian chant. Paraclete is also the exclusive North American distributor of the recordings of the Monastic Choir of St. Peter's Abbey in Solesmes, France, long considered to be a leading authority on Gregorian chant performance.

Learn more about us at our Web site:
www.paracletepress.com, or call us toll-free at
1-800-451-5006

Also by Carmen Butcher

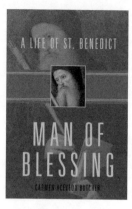

Man of Blessing:
A Life of St. Benedict

176 pages, $21.95, Hardcover
ISBN 10: 1-55725-485-0
ISBN 13: 978-1-55725-485-6

Known to history primarily through Pope Gregory the Great's *Dialogues*, written a century after Benedict's death, this great medieval figure is now made accessible by Carmen Acevedo Butcher. She explores all aspects of his unusual life, illuminating important episodes in the foundation of Western monasticism at the end of the Roman Empire and the beginning of the Middle Ages.

"A succinct, highly readable and comprehensive *Life of St. Benedict*. Carmen Butcher has made a classical spiritual author accessible to a diverse and hungry readership." —John E. Crean, Jr., Ph.D., Obl.S.B.

Incandescence:
365 Readings with the Medieval Mystics

276 pages, $16.95, Paperback
ISBN 10: 1-55725-418-4
ISBN 13: 978-1-55725-418-4

Incandescence offers fresh translations from the writings of famous and not-so-famous mystics— Julian of Norwich, Mechthild of Magdeburg, Catherine of Siena, Hildegard of Bingen, Gertrude of Helfta, Margery Kempe, and others. Each reading includes a meditation, prayer, poem, or song, offering stunning insights on God's divine, mothering love, the guidance of God's light, the sensuality of faith, and more.

"In these pages, the images of the spiritual life are the erotic ones of the feminine experience. They are the stuff of very physically-present women who loved their Lord with a ferocity and passion that could be reported only in those experiences of the flesh. There is peace here in the company of these good women."
    —from the foreword by Phyllis Tickle

Available from most booksellers or through Paraclete Press:
www.paracletepress.com; 1-800-451-5006. Try your local bookstore first.